STAYING IN THE CITY

GS 1181

STAYING IN THE CITY

Faith in the City ten years on

A report by the Bishops'
Advisory Group on Urban Priority Areas

CHURCH HOUSE PUBLISHING
Church House, Great Smith Street, London SW1P 3NZ

ISBN 0 7151 3780 8

Published 1995 by Church House Publishing

Cover design by Leigh Hurlock

Printed in England by The Cromwell Press Ltd, Melksham, Wiltshire

Contents

Introduction   vii

Chapter 1   First in the nation?   1

Chapter 2   Through the eyes of the clergy   33

Chapter 3   First in the Church   37

Chapter 4   The response of the General Synod Boards and Councils   44

Chapter 5   Partners in the city   88

Chapter 6   Staying in the city   109

Appendix 1   Statements of faith and intent   112

Appendix 2   Link officers and diocesan strategies   113

Appendix 3   Who's giving?   120

Appendix 4   Statistics   124

Appendix 5   Bibliography   136

Appendix 6   List of abbreviations   141

Introduction

In the final verses of St Luke's Gospel we are told that the disciples were commanded to 'stay in the city' for it is in the city that they are to receive authority. The Church of England, we believe, only speaks with authority on urban issues because the Church still 'stays in the city'. This has to include the inner cities, urban estates, coalfields and other deprived communities. Martin Luther King jnr. said 'I must be who I am so that you can be who you are; you must be who you are, so that I can be who I am.' The urban Church must be who it is called to be so that we all may know our identity as a national Church – one that commands respect and authority from all in our land. Those who know the Church as an international body, know also of our debt to the multi-cultural urban Church in this land as a bridge into this international communion of saints. To stay, serve and witness in the city then is of the very essence of the Church.

The report *Faith in the City*, published ten years ago, painted a vivid picture of environmental decay and social disintegration in Britain's inner cities. Its powerful mixture of reportage and analysis ensured that, even today, well-thumbed copies can be seen on bookshelves all over the country; not just on well-stacked clergy shelves, but in the homes of all those with a concern for people living in extreme deprivation.

Faced with acute suffering and despair, the report recognised the critical role of the Church in providing hope for all people and especially those living in the most deprived areas of the country.

Ten years on from the publication of the report it is right to ask what difference the report has made. We glibly use the phrase 'Urban Priority Areas', but have the Church and the nation really given *priority* to places of urban deprivation, to the people who live there and the staff who work there? Putting UPAs first? Or squeezing them out when resources are scarce?

These questions are perhaps even more pertinent when addressed to the nation. With the gap between the richest and the poorest ever widening, some have pointed to the emergence of an urban underclass; people dependent on welfare and feeling they have no real stake in society. There is an African proverb which says, 'When there is a thorn in the foot the whole body must bend to pluck it out otherwise it festers and the whole body is poisoned.' We believe that if our country is not to have its national life poisoned in this way it must listen to the voices of those seeking to draw attention to the plight of those in UPAs.

Staying in the City sets out for members of the General Synod and all those with an interest in *Faith in the City*, what the Church of England is now doing in UPAs. In 1995, we face a new situation, both in the Church and the nation, and we have attempted to identify what now needs to be done. The Turnbull Commision has proposed sweeping changes to the central administrative structures of the Church of England. Although many of our observations are directed at particular Boards, these will be equally relevant to whatever structures emerge and indeed some of them mirror concerns voiced in the report. We hope that these observations will inform and contribute to the process of change.

Chapter 1 sets out a digest of recent research into economic and social conditions, which suggests that deprivation now is as severe, if not more so, than ten years ago. We have included in Chapter 2 some initial findings from a clergy attitude survey conducted by Dr Graham Bowpitt of Nottingham Trent University. Further analysis of the results will provide a useful basis for on-going work; for now it identifies some possible trends which will bear closer examination. Chapter 3 provides an overview of developments in the Church, with our comments and this is fleshed out in Chapter 4. Chapter 5 describes the work being done by a number of other church-related organisations. We conclude, in Chapter 6, by offering recommendations for the next ten years and beyond. To help you to interpret the material in your own situation we have included boxed questions which draw attention to some of the local implications.

A great deal of work has gone into this report and I am particularly grateful to all who have been involved in its production: to members of the Synod report steering group and the Advisory Group, Sylvia Clayton, Raymond Tongue from the CBF statistics department, the urban link officers, the Urban Bishops' Panel, the Church Urban Fund, the General Synod Boards and Councils and all other bodies and individuals who contributed to the report.

The Rt Revd Tom Butler
Bishop of Leicester

Chapter 1

First in the nation?

1.1   *Faith in the City* in 1985 cried out, with facts and figures, the multiple economic and social deprivation being suffered by people living in urban priority areas. The report described their poverty and unemployment, lack of adequate housing, health care, social services and educational opportunities, and high incidence of crime – in absolute terms as well as relative to the rest of society. It spelt out why these conditions could not be tolerated by the Church which should become local, participative and outward-looking.

1.2   What has changed in the ten years since then? In this chapter we bring together the findings of a number of surveys relating to these issues, some nationally and some specifically in urban priority areas, published within the last year or so by the Government or independent bodies. Their very number is a measure of the widespread ongoing concern with these issues. They include:

● the major study, *Assessing the Impact of Urban Policy,* undertaken for the Department of the Environment by a team of academics led by Professor Brian Robson and published by HMSO in 1994

● the reports *Urban Trends 1* and *2,* edited by Peter Willmott and published by the Policy Studies Institute in 1992 and 1994

● the *Inquiry into Income and Wealth* by a group convened by the Joseph Rowntree Foundation and chaired by Sir Peter Barclay, a former chairman of the government's Social Security Advisory Committee; also a number of other relevant studies published by the Foundation

● the report *Tackling Inequalities in Health,* based upon a King's Fund seminar chaired by Sir Donald Acheson, a former Chief Medical Officer for England

● *People Need Homes,* the briefing published by the Churches National Housing Coalition and briefing notes on a variety of subjects published by Church Action on Poverty

● the reports of the independent Commission on Social Justice, chaired by Sir Gordon Borrie, QC, and National Commission on Education, chaired by Lord Walton of Detchant

1

- reports on *The Distribution of UK household expenditure: 1972–92* and *Poverty Dynamics in Great Britain* by Steven Webb and Alissa Goodman of the Institute for Fiscal Studies

- the recent report of the House of Commons Education Committee *Performance in City Schools*

- written evidence submitted to the House of Commons Committee on the Environment (including that by the Bishops' Officer for UPAs) in connection with their current inquiry into the Single Regeneration Budget Challenge Fund.

Details of all sources are given in appendix 5. We are grateful to those concerned for permission to reproduce their findings here.

1.3   At the end of each section we invite readers to relate these findings to their own experience.

1.4   At the end of each section we have set out BAGUPA's comments and some questions in boxes, to help readers interpret some of the material in their own contexts. These questions are not exhaustive and we hope that many more will arise during the course of reading. Some of the questions look for an individual response; others relate to the work of parishes, others to the activities of diocesan bodies. Various points are illustrated with short snapshots in tinted boxes.

Wealth . . . and poverty

1.5   One big change over the past ten years is that Britain as a whole is much richer. Between 1979 and 1992 real incomes (i.e. over and above inflation) increased on average by more than one third. This represents a substantial increase in total national resources. What it has been used for has been decided partly by the Government (which has continued to appropriate, through a variety of taxes, nearly half the national income to finance public expenditure) and partly by the choices of the individuals who have become better off.

1.6   Not all have gained equally. This is illustrated by the figure on page 4, which is reproduced from the recent Institute of Fiscal Studies report *The Distribution of UK Household Expenditure: 1979-1992*. It shows changes in real income and in real expenditure over that period, per household member, net of direct tax and housing costs (which eliminates the distorting effect of the replacement of subsidised rents by housing benefit). It measures the change between the position of people who are among, for example, the poorest tenthh of the population in 1979 and the position of those who are among the poorest tenth in 1992. These are by no means the same individuals. Individual people may get richer or poorer from one year to another, for all sorts of reasons, and whole groups may change their relative position – for example there are fewer pensioners among the poorest tenth in 1992 than there were in 1979. What is being measured is changes between the two dates in the composition of our society.

1.7   It will be seen that the average income of those who were in the poorest tenth in 1992 was substantially lower (in real terms) than that of the poorest tenth in 1979, and the average income of those in the second poorest tenth a little lower than that of the second poorest tenth on 1979. For other groups it was higher, the more so the richer the group. The average expenditure of the lowest spending group in 1992 was higher than that of the corresponding group in 1979, and this increase was slightly greater than the increase in the average expenditure of the second lowest spending group. But for other groups the increase, again, was greater the higher spending the group.

1.8   The apparent divergence between the changes measured by income and the changes measured by expenditure is probably due mainly to changes in the composition of the groups. Incomes may be understated, but that would not affect these comparisons over time unless it were a bigger factor in one year than in another. And changes in expenditures may reflect not only changes in incomes but also changes in indebtedness or in amounts invested (which produce further income). But what is clear is that on either measure the gap between rich and poor has grown much wider.

1.9   The Joseph Rowntree Foundation Inquiry Group drew attention to the fact that the gap between rich and poor had grown faster than in any other industrialised country save New Zealand, and was by 1990 wider than at any time since the War. They found no evidence that any beneficial effects that inequality might have on economic growth 'trickled down' to raise the living standards of the poorest; indeed they argued that increasing inequality can damage the economy as well as the social fabric of the country.

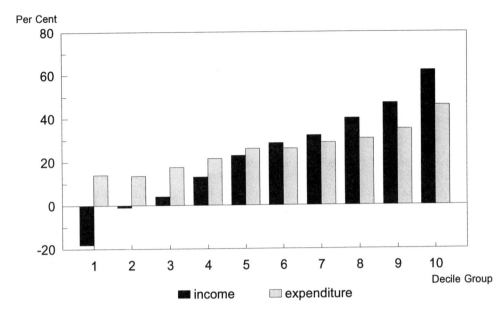

Per Cent

■ income   ▢ expenditure

Changes in expenditure across the expenditure distribution and in income across the income distribution (after housing costs) 1979-1992

1.10   The Inquiry Group suggested that growing inequality was due to a number of cumulative factors:

● more people have become dependent on benefits such as Income Support

● benefits are no longer increased in line with earnings, but with prices

● for those in work, the hourly wages of the lowest paid were in 1992 lower in real terms than they had been in 1975 (whereas median wages grew by 35 per cent and high wages by 50 per cent) and there is a growing group for whom 'self-employment' involves marginal activities generating little income

● the 'automatic' effects of progressive taxes like income tax which tend to slow the growth of inequality have been cancelled out by discretionary tax changes which shifted the burden of taxation from higher to lower and middle income groups.

4

1.11   The Inquiry Group pointed out that this striking polarisation of individual wealth is reflected in growing difference between deprived and affluent neighbourhoods. They drew attention to the following factors:

● parts of the country seem locked in a spiral of decline, but others changed their relative position in the1980s, with the problems of inner London growing substantially

● because council housing is concentrated in particular estates, polarisation of income groups by tenure leads to a concentration of people with low incomes in particular neighbourhoods

● the incomes of certain ethnic minority groups are well below the national average and a large proportion of their populations live in areas of deprivation.

1.12   This is confirmed by *Urban Trends 2*, which found that in 23 of the most deprived local authority districts in Britain the proportion of people dependent on Income Support rose substantially between 1983 and 1993 (to over 28 per cent) compared with only a slight increase (to less than 17 per cent) in the country generally. The report concludes:

A common thread, Wales apart, has been a growing concentration of disadvantage in the inner areas of the great cities of Britain.

Throughout the report we have noted the concentration of deprivation in London and often the same boroughs within it.

Within the North West, the other highly deprived region, the most deprived areas are Liverpool, Knowsley and Manchester. . .

In the West Midlands, Birmingham's problems show up as the most severe.

> *In what ways are you conscious of growing disparities of wealth and poverty? Is this good or bad . . . or inevitable? Are you in any way challenged by it – personally, in your church or in your community?*

Population structure

1.13   What changes have there been in the sort of people living in UPAs? *Urban Trends 2* compared data from the 1981 and 1991 censuses of population for the 36 most deprived local authority areas in Britain:

- the populations of the deprived areas generally fell sharply over the decade compared with other places

- most of these areas, apart from London, contained fewer people senior jobs and more with low skilled jobs than the average; but in general the social class patterns were not dramatically different from those of the country as a whole, and overall the differences narrowed over time

- similarly most of these areas, apart from London, had lower than average proportions of people with educational qualifications, but in most the gap narrowed over time

- households in deprived areas were less likely to have cars, but again the gap narrowed

- minority ethnic populations were concentrated in deprived areas in 1981 and had become more so by 1991

- deprived areas had larger than average proportions of lone-parent households in 1981 and more so in 1991, but co-habitation was no more common than elsewhere in 1991

- the proportion of children under five was larger than average, and increased

- in England and Wales (unlike Scotland) the proportion of elderly people, though it increased over the decade, was smaller in deprived areas than average

- in most of these respects there were wide variations between (and no doubt within) different deprived areas, those in London conspicuously so in terms of class and educational qualifications.

> *What changes have there been in the population of your area over the last ten years or so? Are there more people living round you or fewer? (The local council should be able to tell you.) Are there more or fewer older people, young people, people of working age, members of minority ethnic groups, people living on their own, lone parents or people without means of transport? How does this affect the activities of your church, and your community?*

Employment

1.14   A major factor in deprivation is the level of unemployment. Over Britain as a whole, as measured by the Census of Population, unemployment was much the same in 1991 (9.3 per cent) as it had been in 1981 (9.4 per cent). There were ups and downs in between, and the percentage is currently lower, but the total number unemployed in Britain is still around two million.

1.15   In UPAs *Urban Trends 2* summarised the position as follows:

• the general rate of unemployment, as measured by the population census, in our 36 deprived areas taken together was much higher in 1991 than it had been in 1981, both absolutely and relative to the rest of Britain. The increase was particularly marked in the deprived London boroughs. In only ten of our 36 areas was there a decrease.

• among men the 1991 rate was more than one in six in the 36 areas taken together, and more than one in four in Hackney, in Tower Hamlets, in Knowsley and in Liverpool

• among young men the 1991 rate was more than one in four in the 36 areas taken together, and more than one in three in Hackney, in Knowsley and in Liverpool

• among women the 1991 rate was more than one in ten in the 36 areas taken together, a lower rate than for men but it had increased faster. Among young women the rate was higher than for older women, but had actually fallen slightly since 1981

• From 1991 to 1993 deprived areas in general were less affected by the recession than their surrounding areas, but the resulting improvement in their relative position was halted or reversed from early 1993 onwards as other areas began to recover. Because of the particular severity of the recession in the south east, unemployment in the 13 deprived London boroughs taken together continued to increase faster than the rest of Britain throughout the period.

- Within our deprived areas the particular localities covered by government task forces, for various periods since 1986, in general showed some improvement relative to the rest of these areas from 1989 or 1990 onwards. But in half of them this improvement was halted or reversed after 1993, again suggesting a link to cyclical factors rather than the existence of task forces.

1.16   *Urban Trends* also found that within generally declining populations the number economically active declined even faster as people moved out to take a job elsewhere, or to search for one. The proportion of part-time employees increased much less than elsewhere and remained below the national average. Self-employment increased more rapidly than elsewhere, but also remained below average.

How many unemployed people are there in your area? How long have they been without a job? What is it like to be unemployed if you are a man or a woman over 50? Or a young person under 25? What effect is the fear of unemployment having on people? Can you or your church or your community do anything more to help people while they are unemployed, or help them to find jobs?

Housing

1.17   The Churches National Housing Coalition (CNHC) have recently issued a number of briefing papers on the housing situation in the country as a whole. The first, on homeless families, makes the following points:

- every working day, on average, more than 1,000 households apply to local councils for help on the grounds of homelessness

- in the past ten years, well over a million households in Britain have been registered as homeless by local authorities, adding up to more than three million people – half of them children

- homelessness is a national problem affecting large numbers of people and different kinds of area from inner cities to rural villages

- homelessness is not a passing phenomenon – it has been increasing and spreading for the past 30 years, but took a stronger hold in the 1980s and early 1990s

- the critical problem is a shortage of affordable rented housing.

1.18   The second CNHC briefing paper, on youth homelessness, said:

- young people currently have no right to housing

- it is estimated that there are up to 150,000 homeless young people in Britain today

- since 1988 agencies working with homeless people have reported a drastic increase in the number of 16 to 17 year olds who are becoming homeless.

1.19   A third paper, on the need for rented homes, made the following points:

- several studies over the past five years have concluded that something of the order of 100,000 new social rented dwellings in England are required each year if housing needs are to be met by the end of the decade

- the most recent study, commissioned by the National Federation of Housing Associations, indicated that 124,000 additional homes would need to be found in the social rented sector each year for the next ten years. The actual planned output (1994-97) is 53,000.

1.20   The CNHC draw attention to the Government's announced intention to introduce legislation to end local authorities' duty to provide homeless families with permanent housing and make the following points:

- the proposed legislation will not alter the facts set out above: the need (and the families) will still be there

- research commissioned in 1989 by the Department of the Environment itself found that the image of well-informed, demanding and undeserving people making unreasonable claims on the local authority is far from the picture revealed by the survey

- a majority of lone parents with young children who become homeless have experienced the breakdown of a marriage or other

9

partnership. Their average age is mid-to-late 20s, and about half of them previously had a permanent home of their own.

1.21   Another government proposal, to limit Housing Benefit if the rent is higher than the mid-point for the locality, is questioned in a report *How Housing Benefit can work for community care*, published by the Joseph Rowntree Foundation. The author, Steve Griffiths, says:

> Whilst reform is overdue, the Government's plans assume that tenants, when Housing Benefit has been restricted, will be able to negotiate with landlords to achieve a more reasonable rent. Where people are in poor health it is clear that this is unfair, unrealistic and quite contrary to the objectives of community care.

1.22   As for the housing position in UPAs in particular, *Urban Trends 2* included a substantial chapter on housing and homelessness based on census material, official statistics and Government surveys of house conditions. It drew the following conclusions:

- council housing, in 1991 still a much larger element in deprived areas than elsewhere, declined sharply over the preceding decade, and the new homes built by housing associations have done little to make up for the fall. The total stock of low-cost social housing – which is what its poorer residents need – has therefore continued to decline

- homelessness has consequently continued at high levels particularly in London and some other cities. In about a third of the deprived areas the levels of homelessness and the extent of placement in temporary accommodation have fallen, but in most deprived areas both proportions have risen, and there is no general evidence of improvement

- as well as a fall in house construction in deprived areas, much work is needed on their existing stock. Our examination of the work done under Government improvement programmes for council housing in England shows that these have not been given higher priority in deprived areas than elsewhere.

- the house condition survey shows that, although the proportion of vacant dwellings fell in most places between 1986 and 1991, it fell less in the deprived areas than nationally

- overcrowding fell everywhere between 1981 and 1991, but it fell less in the most deprived areas than in their regions and in the country as a whole, and in 1991 it remained more common in deprived areas

- more households in deprived areas than elsewhere lacked an inside WC of their own and/or a bath or shower of their own. The proportion without exclusive use of an indoor WC fell between 1981 and 1991 at a similar rate to the national rate, but the proportion without bath or shower fell more in the deprived areas than elsewhere.

1.23   Research by Anne Power and Rebecca Tunstall of the London School of Economics, funded by the Joseph Rowntree Foundation, in what were 20 of Britain's worst housing estates shows that the massive refurbishments and new tenant-oriented policies launched in the early 1980s (and advocated in *Faith in the City*) have produced significant improvements in physical conditions, more community facilities, less litter and fewer empty properties. But with increasing economic and social disadvantage the fears of social breakdown from concentrations of the needy and vulnerable were so acute that specialised local measures to reinforce community stability – and continued relatively low-level investment – were constantly necessary.

1.24   In a recent speech to the Chartered Institute of Housing, the Archbishop of Canterbury said:

> We have in many ways a great opportunity to make further progress because many of the issues I have discussed today are not the subject of party political dog-fighting. Hardly anybody thinks the best way forward lies either in the free play of market forces or a return to mass municipal housing. There is a great deal of good research and a significant degree of consensus about elements of the way forward.

> There is a need for a healthier and decent quality private rented sector, kick-started by purposeful Government intervention; an onslaught on housing scarcity for people at the bottom of the heap; a mix of tenures and types of social housing, avoiding excessive concentrations of poverty; continuing downward pressure on tax breaks for most owner-occupiers, and a redeployment of those resources to more sensible priorities. We must have action

on the Housing Benefit poverty trap; full-blooded commitment to the regeneration of the UPAs, involving strong voluntary sector participation as well as public and private agencies; support for regeneration from mainstream public expenditure and rating policies, as well as specific urban initiatives such as the Single Regeneration Budget.

In all this, there is substantial convergence of informed opinion, and the chance of a healthy critical mass for policies of regeneration, reform and hope.

> *How many people in your area are homeless or not properly housed? (The local council should be able to tell you the number of families, and there may be voluntary bodies who know about single homeless people.) What sort of ages are they? Do they have other problems? Can you or your church or your local community do anything more to help them, with temporary accommodation or a permanent home?*

Health

1.25   On the health of the country generally the report of the independent Commission on Social Justice made the following points:

- average life expectancy rose by two years between 1981 and 1991, infant mortality continues to fall and preventable diseases have been virtually eradicated

- yet throughout the United Kingdom growing inequality of income is being matched by growing inequality of health

- a baby whose father is an unskilled manual worker is one and a half times more likely to die before the age of one as the baby of a manager or professional employee

- as British children grow up, the poorest children are twice as likely as those from social class I to die from a respiratory illness, more than four times as likely to be killed in a traffic accident, and more than six times as likely to die in a house fire

- among men aged between 45 and 64, unskilled manual workers are nearly three times as likely as professionals to suffer from a long standing illness which limits their activity

- not only are unemployed people much more likely to suffer a chronic illness or disability, but a middle-aged man made redundant or taking early retirement is twice as likely to die within five years as a man who stays at work

- unemployed men are between ten and fifteen times more likely to attempt suicide, and the suicide rate among young men doubled between 1983 and 1990.

1.26   Reviewing the available statistics on health in deprived areas *Urban Trends 2* said:

- deprived areas still have higher standardised mortality ratios than elsewhere, and in two-thirds of the deprived areas in England and Wales the gap has widened

- perinatal and infant mortality rates have continued to fall in most deprived areas as in England and Wales, but there has been a recent upward trend in some, and the levels have remained higher than average in most

- the 1991 census figures on the proportions of people with a long-standing illness or disability show larger than average proportions in all the deprived areas in Britain outside London.

1.27   In his foreword to the King's Fund report *Tackling Inequalities in Health* (based on a seminar held at Ditchley Park in 1993 and published in 1995) Sir Donald Acheson, formerly the Government's Chief Medical Officer for England, wrote:

> The wide and increasing social differential in premature illness and death in Britain should be a matter for serious public concern. In 1995 it seems almost commonplace to repeat what has been known for at least twenty years . . . namely that in this country death rates at most ages (including childhood) are two or three times as high in lower as in upper social classes and that among the least well-off this leads to an attenuation of life of at least eight years together with a corresponding increased burden of ill health and disability. Today the question is not whether these facts are valid but who cares and what can be done

about them. In the circumstances it is particularly unfortunate that the issue has become a party political football.
. . .

We now see that any successful effort to reduce inequalities in health must be based on a broad range of actions involving almost every aspect of society. The approach to a number of the policies which must be considered, such as the redistribution of income, the creation of jobs, investment in new and improved housing (here the report argues that the funding problem is not as problematical as is often thought) and the health impact assessment, is controversial across the political parties; others – including further sanctions on tobacco, the establishment of pre-school education and better child care – are less so. But at present, sadly, there is little evidence that any of the parties sees inequalities in health as a priority issue.

> *Does your area have any particular health problems? Are your local health facilities – GPs, clinics, hospitals – better or worse than elsewhere? (Ask any people you know who live in very different sorts of places, and check with your local health authority.) Is voluntary help needed and, if so, could you or your church or local community do anything more?*

Social services

1.28   In UPAs as in the country generally, local authority social services have been under great pressure. There has been no recent independent comprehensive review comparable with those in other fields. However, the Audit Commission and the Social Services Inspectorate of the Department of Health are currently consulting interested parties on the process and content of joint reviews of social services authorities. It is intended to review each authority once every five years. No timetable, nor order of priority for review, has yet been announced.

> *Will you, your church or your local community have comments to make when the Audit Commission carry out their review of your local social services?*

Education and training

1.29   The last decade has seen a range of government initiatives, some particularly in UPAs, concerned with vocational education and training aimed at preparing young people for the demands of working life in a rapidly changing society. An evaluation by the National Foundation for Educational Research, published in the journal of the Policy Studies Institute, *Policy Studies, Autumn 1994*, concluded:

> The picture, unsurprisingly, is a mixed one. On the one hand, there is evidence of real change and improvement brought about by particular programmes and initiatives. Students' motivation, their satisfaction with school, their access to information and opportunities and even their ability to be 'lifelong learners' all seem to have been enhanced; links between schools, colleges, the local community and the world of work have been firmly established and continue to develop. . .

> On the other hand, there remain many substantive issues and problems to be resolved. The evidence suggests two major areas for action, both requiring a longer-term perspective than the lifetime of an initiative can always provide. On the supply side, there is a need for more work to be done on understanding and managing the motivation and 'learning culture' of young people – particularly the low-achievers, the under-achievers and the disadvantaged; and for more help to be given to them in realising their post-16 options . . .

> On the demand side, there is a need to ensure that the rhetoric of the highly trained, highly skilled workforce of the future is matched by the practical opportunities offered to all young people, through work experience, careers guidance and post-16 education and training placements . . .

1.30   A National Commission on Education was set up in 1991 by the British Association for the Advancement of Science and others, funded by the Paul Hamlyn Foundation and chaired by Lord Walton of Detchant. Its report, published in 1993, included the following paragraph:

Many State-maintained schools achieve excellent results by any standards. On the other hand results in deprived areas are sometimes disappointing. This may not be any fault of the schools, and in fact there are many schools which do well in discouraging circumstances. The fact is that the dice are loaded against any school in such areas. As a result, a cycle of failure may set in which is self-reinforcing: abler pupils and more active parents seek places elsewhere, resources decline as funds follow pupils away and good staff are increasingly hard to recruit.

1.31   This was based on research into standards of education in deprived urban areas undertaken for the Commission by Professor Michael Barber of Keele University. He summarised his findings as follows:

Standards of education in Britain's deprived urban areas are too low, as demonstrated by GCSE results, assessments at age seven, and HMI reports.

Not only are spending cuts having a detrimental effect but recent reforms are encouraging the tendency of markets to redistribute resources from the weak to the strong.

Individual schools can buck trends only in the short term. LEAs' powers are too constrained for them to tackle successfully and strategically the educational problems of deprived urban areas. A national strategy is urgently required to challenge educational disadvantage in these areas and to build on the many examples of good practice around the country.

A range of possible solutions for raising standards in deprived urban areas is proposed including:

● real growth in spending at small but predictable annual increments over a long time scale, with resources distributed towards areas of greatest need and linked to reform targets

- a local organisation to co-ordinate child-centred services, to support schools, to promote innovation and experiment, and to co-ordinate business, education and community involvement, intervening where a school consistently fails according to recognised criteria

- community-oriented strategic school development plans, and recognition and development of the potential of teachers, other staff and other adults in the community

- universally available child care and nursery education, primary schools concentrating on basic skills, a range of strategies to improve pupil motivation in secondary schools, a wider range of after-school educational opportunities, and encouragement of specialisation of schools (with a return to selection by overall academic ability being ruled out)

- continuation of the improved participation in post-compulsory education.

1.32   The conclusions of *Urban Trends 2* regarding education and training in deprived areas are as follows:

- local authorities in the English deprived areas have generally succeeded in moving closer than those elsewhere to providing nursery education for all children under five. But in those areas, and elsewhere, the goal remains a long way off, and the figures show that in some deprived areas it may have begun to recede in recent years

- pupil/teacher ratios fell between 1981 and 1992, not only in England as a whole but in some deprived areas. But over the longer term and more recently, the ratio rose (class sizes increased) in about half the deprived areas

- examination results improved over time in most English deprived areas, although the level of success remained below average in nearly all

- the proportions staying on at school increased in English deprived areas as they did elsewhere, but in many of them the level remained low and the comparison with average levels worsened

- over the last three years there have been improvements in the outcomes from Employment Training and Youth Training among leavers from urban programme areas in nearly all regions. These have often been greater than the improvements in the surrounding regions. Also, in particular years, UPA leavers in some regions did better than the regional average. But the ET and YT leavers from UPAs in all regions did less well in finding jobs than other leavers in their region.

1.33   In July 1995 the House of Commons Education Committee published a report on their inquiry into *Performance in City Schools* (to which the Bishops' Officer for UPAs submitted evidence). Their conclusions and recommendations included the following:

- it is clear from the evidence we have received that there needs to be an increase in the provision of quality nursery education in city areas

- if parents have low expectations of what their children can achieve, and of the value of education, schools will have a substantial burden to carry. This is particularly the case in deprived urban areas, where there are already many other obstacles placed in the way of successful school performance. Furthermore, in such areas, the school is often the most important institution that can help children achieve their full potential . . . While we recognise the many pressures on families in deprived urban areas, there is no excuse for parents' wilful disregard of their children's education

- it is important to find some means of speaking to parents in their own language if that is not English. It is also important to avoid discomfiting parents whose English is non-standard

- the forging of improved links cannot be managed by the Education Welfare Service alone, but the EWS, in co-operation with the school, should give a high priority to improving these links . . . The effort that has to go into this process must be recognised in funding arrangements

- we commend the vital work of the Education Welfare Service, and recommend that local and national government ensure that it is resourced on an equitable basis with those other local services which are rightly seen as indispensable. This is particularly relevant to achievement in city schools

- schools, if they are to assist the children to develop fully, must take account of both the culture of the children's home background and the British-European cultures . . . Nevertheless, such accommodation should not compromise the crucial task of ensuring that all children, whatever their ethnic background, learn to speak and read English

- we believe that the paramount task in city primary schools – actually in all primary schools, but more difficult to achieve in those in deprived urban areas – is to teach children to read and write . . . Those children whose home tongue is English may also have specific language needs that must be met if they are to gain from schooling as they should

- new ways must be found to encourage able, experienced teachers to work in city schools and remain long enough to provide stability and continuity

- extra support must be provided for non-teaching, but important and essential, social responsibilities to allow teachers in both secondary and primary schools actually to teach

- we recognise that various forms of organisation and range of teaching methods should be in use in schools in inner cities as else where . . . The choice should be influenced not by fashion, but by fitness for purpose

- crime is a drain on financial and staff resources. It is not suffered, to such an extent, by schools in less challenging environments as it is by schools in deprived urban areas

- it is clear that schools in the most disadvantaged areas of the country will continue to need to take special measures that will in turn involve a higher level of financial – and other – support than is required by schools in more favourable areas . . . But it is also clear that making the best use of the cash available involves the proper targeting and management of money, and rigorous monitoring of the effectiveness of the outputs achieved by spending it

- we remain concerned about the effect the Single Regeneration Budget may have on programmes designed to ensure that children who do not speak English as their first language become proficient in English . . . The SRB system must ensure that adequate funding continues to be made available to Section 11-type projects to support all such children in learning English

- we commend the success of the GEST (Grants for Education Support and Training) initiative, which has provided support for focused initiatives which have had direct and quantifiable benefits for children's education

- we recommend that the current level of funding for Compacts (£4.6 million in 1995-96) be maintained in future years

- the downward spiral of some schools, even if other schools are flourishing, cannot be of benefit to the education system. We are in no doubt that action must be taken, and taken quickly, to stop any school sliding towards ineffectiveness.

> *Is there a need for more nursery education in your area? How do your local schools rate in examination 'league tables' and in the opinion of parents, teachers and pupils? Do they have any particular problems? Could you or your church or local community help?*

Order and law

1.34   *Urban Trends 2* reported:

- the British Crime Surveys show that levels of crime are higher in inner city areas than in others, and that they rose in such areas about as much as they did elsewhere between 1983 and 1991

- this fear of crime is higher in inner city areas than other areas, but between 1983 and 1991 this fear fell more in such areas than elsewhere.

1.35   In her Cantor Lecture to the Royal Society of Arts in April 1993, Vivien Stern, Director of the National Association for the Care and Resettlement of Offenders said:

> Many questions about the relationship between crime and social policy are unanswered. But the weight of evidence internationally points to certain propositions. Weakening community support structures, reducing opportunities for young people, widening inequalities and leaving vulnerable families to fend for themselves will lead to crime.

Decisions are regularly being taken with no attempt made to test them for their crime-producing potential. The recent decision to phase out the Urban Programme, which for years supported small local projects providing a lifeline for many families in difficulties, is taken without reference to the contribution it will make to the crime rate. The decision to remove income support from 16 and 17 year olds and to offer them instead a place on a Youth Training Scheme has undoubtedly had an effect on levels of crime amongst young people. But arguments that this would happen did not influence the decision.

The chance to learn a skill and then to gain a place in the labour market is widely regarded as one of the basic factors leading to stability for individuals and families. Yet every year, policies on training for employment mean that the schemes which cater for the most disadvantaged people are further reduced and their capacity to deal with difficult people eroded.

1.36   Somewhat similarly, John Wells of the University of Cambridge wrote in the Economic Report of the Employment Policy Institute in February 1995:

Cross-section evidence from 41 police force areas in England and Wales in 1992 confirms the strong association between property crime and unemployment. The fact is the nation's unemployment black spots (Cleveland, Merseyside, Northumbria, Greater Manchester, South Yorkshire, West Midlands, Greater London, South Wales) are also its crime black spots.

One objection to this result is that unemployment may be acting as a proxy for numerous other aspects of social and economic deprivation (e.g. poor housing, low educational attainment, etc.) making it difficult to identify the specific contribution of unemployment. However, the reason our great urban conurbations are the nation's crime spots reflects poor regional/national economic performance, particularly rapid de-industrialisation in recent years. Revitalisation of these economies must surely be the key to reducing crime both directly through its beneficial labour market effects and through reducing other dimensions of deprivation.

> *Is crime better or worse than it used to be in your area? Are you and other people more or less afraid of it? What do you think has made a difference? Can you or your church or your local community do anything more about it, either directly or by contacting the police, your local councillors or MPs? Who is looking after the victims of crime?*

Urban policy

1.37   Over the years since publication of *Faith in the City* the Government's urban policy has been characterised by a plethora of initiatives and a shortage of resources.

1.38   The Urban Programme, Urban Development Corporations, Enterprise Zones, Urban Development Grant, Urban Regeneration Grant, City Grant, City Action Teams, Estate Action, Safer Cities, the Ethnic Minorities Business Initiative, English Estates and Task Forces each had their brief moment of glory before being swept up into the launch of Action for Cities in 1988. This in turn was followed in 1991 by City Challenge and in 1992 by the launch of the Urban Regeneration Agency.

1.39   The government then commissioned from Professor Robson and his team from the Universities of Manchester, Durham and John Moores, Liverpool a major study, published in 1994 as *Assessing the Impact of Urban Policy*. This surveyed a sample of 123 districts, including all the 57 districts which had been covered by the original Urban Programme and others as 'controls'.

1.40   The report found that in these districts total expenditure on programmes, which were eventually brought within the framework of Action for Cities, increased in cash terms from £156m in 1979/80 to £1321m in 1989/90 ten years later – an impressive increase by more than eightfold. Over the same period and for the same authorities expenditure under the Housing Investment Programme fell from £1,628m to £827m and under the Rate Support Grant rose from £4,225m to £6,304m. Inclusive of Regional Selective Assistance and European funds, total expenditure increased from £6,047m in 1979/80 to £8,650m in 1989/90, an increase of 43 per cent in cash terms. Over the same period retail prices approximately doubled.

1.41   We quote in full the report's summary of its findings on inputs and outcomes:

> Inputs: a general point which emerges from the pattern of expenditure of the AfC (Action for Cities) resources over the course of the 1980s is the lack of fit between the classification of authorities as urban priority areas and the amounts of resource that they received per capita. While many elements of AfC expenditure were never intended to apply solely to the 57 UPAs, there nevertheless appears to be some ambiguity about the principle of targeting a limited set of authorities. This is compounded by the changes over time in funding; some places which experienced the largest percentage reductions in their overall per capita assistance were UPAs – and in many cases some of the 'worst' UPAs. Equally, looking at a wider definition of resources (the two mainstream programmes of Housing Investment allocations and Revenue Support Grant, whose resources are much larger than AfC), it is clear that in the 1980s there were considerable reductions, especially in HIP allocations, to many UPA authorities.
>
> Outcomes: a mixed picture emerges from the outcome measures. First, there are indications of deteriorating conditions in the UPAs over the period as a whole. Some of the indicators show a worsening position for the UPAs. The ratio of long-term unemployed to all unemployed (LT:U), for example, shows a widening gap as between the UPAs, marginals and comparators; thereby suggesting a deterioration of the areas with the worst conditions. Rates of new-firm formation also suggest that UPAs do somewhat worse than other authorities. On the other hand, there are also indications of areas of improvement; both the unemployment rate and the long-term unemployment rate taken separately, for example, show a narrowing gap. Taken together with the deterioration in the LT:U ratio, this implies that, while the UPAs were experiencing relative improvements as far as unemployment and long-term

unemployment as a whole were concerned, amongst the unemployed in UPA areas, higher proportions were long-term unemployed, thereby signifying an increasing degree of concentration of the most disadvantaged. There is nevertheless evidence in the improvements for the separate unemployment data that policy may have had a positive economic impact.

1.42   The report's general conclusions are summarised as follows:

The pattern that emerges, both for employment opportunities and residential attractiveness, is very mixed. There has been beneficial change – some of it relative, some absolute. . . But in the most deprived areas. . . policy has not been able to make significant inroads. The biggest and most deprived urban areas have generally experienced a continuing deterioration.

1.43   The report drew the following policy conclusions:

- there are clear indications of the importance of creating effective coalitions of 'actors' within localities and that these are most likely to result from the development of structures and mechanisms which encourage or require long-term collaborative partnerships

- local authorities – in their newly emergent roles as enablers and facilitators – need to be given greater opportunities to play a significant part in such coalitions

- local communities equally need to be given opportunities to play roles in such coalitions. The evidence of increasing polarisation suggests the need for specific resources to address the scope for community capacity-building within deprived areas

- there remains a need to improve the coherence of programmes both across and within Government departments. This requires a greater emphasis on the identification of strategic objectives which can guide departmental priorities. Area targeting has played an important part in those cases where separate programmes have been successfully linked so as to create additionality (i.e. the effect of the whole has been greater than the sum of its parts) thereby suggesting the value of giving yet greater emphasis to area-based approaches. Such creative linkage of policy instruments would be helped by increasing the flexibility of expenditure through a more relaxed approach to virement

- an important part of such coherence must derive from less ambiguity in the targeting of resources. There is a strong argument for the development of an urban budget which might be administered at regional level so as to reflect the varying constraints and opportunities across different regions and to improve co-ordination across programmes and departments.

> *One inner city neighbourhood shared local shopping facilities with another until the latter became a City Challenge area. As the shopping precinct was being levelled ready for redevelopment, the residents were disappearing from the City Challenge area as it was cleared. But just across the road people were staying put. Nobody seemed to have given much thought to where they might shop in the years in between while the developers try to find a major supermarket chain sufficiently committed to the site to be able to sustain the whole venture. The wait goes on. Have you experienced any similar lack of co-ordination? What might be done about it?*

The Single Regeneration Budget

1.44   In the light of Professor Robson's study the Government announced in 1993 the introduction of a Single Regeneration Budget to operate in the following financial year. This brought within the scope of a single bidding process the budgets of Action for Cities and a number of other programmes previously administered by separate Government departments.

1.45   *Urban Trends 2* comments:

- the policy has many welcome features, particularly the emphasis on local initiative and partnership. But there are two major worries about the SRB. The first and most important is the cut in resources that came with it. Total spending on the elements now being incorporated into the SRB is being reduced from £1.6 billion last year (1993/94) to £1.4 billion in the current year (1994/95) and £1.3 billion in 1995/96 (the SRB's first year of operation). Most of the money is earmarked for current programmes, leaving only £100m for new bids

- the second worry is that the SRB is open to bids from any area, not just the most deprived, so that the reduced resources are being more widely spread, and the increased emphasis on competition and cost-effectiveness may leave some of the most needy areas with no help.

1.46   That those worries were justified seems to have been borne out by the further reduction in resources since announced for subsequent years and an analysis of the first round of bidding commissioned by the Urban Forum sponsored by the National Council for Voluntary Organisations. This found, *inter alia*:

- SRB bidding has been a very mixed and variable process across the country for the voluntary and community sector

- much of SRB bidding activity was driven by cuts in public funding. Most TECs (Training and Enterprise Councils) and LAs (local authorities) have been driven by the desire to replace 'lost' or 'vulnerable' funding which they consider to be rightly theirs. This has often led to the desire for 'on paper' partnerships to be stronger than the will to act in full partnership. Equally, the private sector, with its levered funds has been a more attractive partner than the local community.

1.47   Further comment on the SRB is given by Phil Shiner of the University of Central England in a study published by the Centre for Local and Economic Strategies. He has five major criticisms:

- accountability . . . the informality of the bidding process means that there are opportunities for patronage

- issues of social equity . . . there are some startling omissions. Relatively deprived urban areas such as Bolton, Walsall, Leicester and Nottingham receive nothing, but Bedford, Hertfordshire and Eastbourne benefit from nearly £7 million . . .

- SRB is inefficient: round one produced 256 losing partnerships. The costs of preparing bids are in six figures, besides raised expectations.

- a major threat to housing capital programmes. In 1993/94 approximately £80 million Estate Action funds were available for new housing schemes compared with the Institute of Housing's estimate of a paltry £15 million SRB money in 1995/96

- the hidden reductions contained within SRB mean that the problems of concentrations of socially excluded groups in urban areas must worsen.

> *Under the Government's Estate Action Programme a local authority began essential redevelopment work on a medium-sized inner city council estate. Two-thirds of the estate is being tackled under a rolling programme lasting several years. The fate of the final third is uncertain because funding now comes through the SRB and nothing was awarded in the first round. Residents are worried that that part of the estate will become a 'sink'. The head-teachers and governors of local primary schools are already struggling with the budget implications of temporarily falling rolls due to the redevelopment and any further delay will make their situation worse. A new CUF-supported community centre in the heart of the remaining third fears for its ability to secure funding in the future because of the uncertainty. And no-one knows anything for sure. Do you know of projects which have suffered from the uncertainty of future funding? Could grant-making bodies do more to provide secure, long-term funding while preserving flexibility for new projects?*

1.48   Following the introduction of the Single Regeneration Budget, the Church of England has established a network of link officers and bishops whose task it is to develop close links with the new regional offices, thus making them aware of the role faith communities have to play in urban regeneration. The Church is keen to stress that lasting change can only be brought about when local people are fully involved in schemes to regenerate their neighbourhoods; it presses for capacity building of voluntary groups to be built into regeneration programmes. Consultation is at present usually token; we should be aiming at full participation.

Have there been any urban redevelopment programmes – buildings, training schemes, community centres, traffic schemes, etc. – where you live or where you work?

Was it money well spent in your opinion? Were local people consulted? Have you or your church or your local community any further ideas for improving things for people living or working in the area? Have you had any experience of applying for a grant from the Church Urban Fund, the Single Regeneration Budget, any other funds that may be available from the local council, Government departments, local businesses or charitable trusts? Is it worth a try?

Conclusions

1.49   In a paper presented to the Social Policy Association Conference in July 1993 and published in H Jones and J Lansley's book, *Social Policy in the City*, Dr Graham Bowpitt of Nottingham Trent University examined the impact of *Faith in the City* on public policy and summed up as follows:

> Part 3 of *Faith in the City*, which takes up more than half the report, is nothing short of a manifesto for the regeneration of British urban life. Recommendations included the expansion of revenue support grant to local authorities, and other current urban initiatives such as the Urban Programme and the Community Programme, greater partnership between central and local Government and local people in developing responses to urban deprivation, various job creation measures, policies to improve the income of the unemployed, an expanded public housing programme and redistribution of housing finance, and the better resourcing of care in the community. None of these proposals were original in themselves, but together they commanded public respect and attention well beyond the Church's own membership because they were the product of a genuinely disinterested concern for the most disadvantaged at a time when Government was perceived to be uncaring and all other sources of political opposition were

weak and divided. It might not be too much of an exaggeration to say that this manifesto captured the mood of the nation. . .

Notwithstanding the initial critical reaction of some Government spokespeople, what effect has *Faith in the City* had on urban policy? Though the 'call to action' was addressed more broadly to the nation as a whole, the bulk of the recommendations demand a policy response from Government. But we look in vain for any immediate impact. A superficial look at the Conservative Party manifesto at the 1987 general election reveals some sort of commitment to just four of the 23 recommendations to the Government. Yet, as Mrs. Thatcher's celebrated statement on election night indicates, the inner city had assumed a higher place on the government's policy-making agenda. The report had elicited a response, though it wasn't exactly the one for which the Commission might have hoped, as any detailed examination of the Government's 'Action for Cities' programme shows.

In its five year review of progress, *Living Faith in the City*, the Archbishop's Advisory Group put a charitable gloss on this dissonance between Government policy and the aspirations of *Faith in the City* claiming that it 'is not for lack of public commitment on the part of central Government to the needs of the inner cities'. But a comparative survey makes depressing reading. Against the report's call for an increase in Rate Support Grant especially to UPAs, an expansion of the Urban programme, a new partnership between central and local government, a new commitment to the funding of the voluntary sector, and a greater priority for outer estates, the Advisory Group noted a decline in real terms in revenue support grant and the Urban Programme, the continued sidestepping of local authorities in favour of big business, the loss of funding for the voluntary sector with the collapse of the Community Programme, and a continued indifference towards outer estates.

In the face of this, an ever optimistic Advisory Group applauded the establishment of institutional links between Church and Government with policy-making implications. The hope was that, where policy cannot be changed, it can at least be influenced.

But the impression is gained of oases of influence in a sea of Government indifference. The chapters in *Living Faith in the City* which review progress in social policy give the distinct impress that the Government has, in many cases, done the very opposite of the recommendations of *Faith in the City* and it is significant that the Advisory Group's own recommendations are all addressed to the Church. This is all the more critical for the fact that *Faith in the City* attached a lot of importance to the need for urban deprivation to be attacked along a broad front. It is not a localised, residual problem amenable to selectively focused solutions alone. Problems of structural injustice demand wide-ranging solutions, and the report frequently documents the extent to which urban policy can be undermined by retrenchment in other policy programmes.

Does this therefore mean that *Faith in the City* has failed? I believe that there are good grounds for answering 'no'. The first criterion by which the report's impact is to be judged is whether the Church has acted as an effective political opposition on urban affairs. Although it is hard to point to specific changes of policy arising from *Faith in the City*, the Government now feels obliged to take a religious perspective seriously in its policy deliberations, even to the point of setting up machinery to give expression to this. The main reason for this is that the Church has earned the right to be heard, partly because of the rigour with which it undertook the research on which its own proposals were based, but mainly because it is prepared to put its money where its mouth is and revive its own active involvement in inner city life. As the Bishop of Leicester put it 'we are there, living and working in every corner of every city and every housing estate'.

1.50   From this mass of data and comment on economic and social developments over the last decade in the nation generally and in deprived urban areas in particular the following points stand out:

- urban deprivation is, generally speaking, as bad if not worse than it was ten years ago, posing a growing threat to the social and economic health of the nation as a whole

- there has been a worrying concentration of severe deprivation in the centres and outer estates of the country's biggest cities

- this has occurred despite numerous special programmes and projects by national and local Government, the private sector, voluntary bodies (including the churches) and the local communities themselves

- there have nonetheless been some successes in some particular places and more widely on some aspects of the problem, such as physical refurbishment, which give some grounds for hope for the future

- consensus has grown around the twin themes put forward in *Faith in the City* ten years ago:

  1   the need for an integrated approach to the problems of multiple deprivation

  2   the need in seeking solutions to listen to the voices of the local community.

- despite a one-third increase in national resources over the past ten years, total public expenditure in UPAs during the 1980s fell substantially.

- many UPAs experienced considerable reductions in resources for mainstream programmes (especially housing)

- some UPAs, including some of the most deprived, experienced large percentage reductions in overall *per capita* assistance even under programmes designed specifically for urban regeneration

- most recently, the Single Regeneration Budget offers less money than the programmes it replaced, despite covering a wider area, and is set to reduce in real terms.

> *Do you agree that these are the main conclusions? Do they accord with your own experience? What do you think are the most important things that need doing over the next ten years – by the Government and other public authorities; by private business; by voluntary bodies and local community groups; by churches? What can you do?*

BAGUPA comment:

1.51   In chapter 6, we recommend that the disturbing findings of independent research in the several areas of social and economic policy described in this chapter should be pursued with Government by General Synod through its appropriate Boards, Councils and networks.

Chapter 2

Through the eyes of the clergy

2.1   This is an interim report of a survey comparing the attitudes and ministerial experiences of UPA and non-UPA clergy undertaken as a follow-up of one by Gallup ten years ago as part of the preparation of the original *Faith in the City* report. The aim then was to survey 'the background, organisational structure and attitudes of clergy working in parishes in deprived parts of inner cities or outer estates, known as Urban Priority Areas (UPAs), compared to other areas in England.'

2.2   This latest survey sets out to produce results which can be compared with those of the original survey, and the sampling methods and questions have tried to reflect this. However, this follow-up survey has the additional aim of reviewing the impact of the *Faith in the City* recommendations on parish life and ministry, and some new questions have been asked accordingly.

2.3   As before, a sample of 400 clergy were approached, half serving in UPAs, half in non-UPAs. But whereas in the first survey, all were interviewed, this is mainly a postal survey, with a planned follow-up by interview of 10% of the sample. This interim report is based on the replies so far received to the postal survey from about half those approached, i.e. 100 UPA clergy and 90 non-UPA clergy. This included a proportionate sample of women clergy.

2.4   Our intention is to publish the full and detailed results of the survey at a later date; the results will help church bodies and all with a concern for UPAs to plan and identify new priorities for action.

2.5   At this half-way point, conclusions drawn must necessarily be tentative, but correlations with the earlier survey and with other evidence suggest a reasonable degree of reliability. We have, at this point, not drawn any conclusions about the particular attitudes and experiences of women, from what is naturally a small sample.

2.6   Subject to these limitations, several general points emerge. More clergy perceive levels of deprivation to have risen than fallen in all parishes, a perception which is borne out by most studies of deprivation over the past ten years. However, what might be surprising is that substantially more UPA clergy than non-UPA believed levels of deprivation to have fallen in their parishes.

2.7   It appears from the figures to date that clergy, who are often uniquely placed to observe the problems of a locality, believe that the problems of multiple deprivation which persist in certain areas of our cities have scarcely altered in ten years, getting neither better nor worse. The most acute problems are still those of unemployment, marital breakdown, burglary and vandalism, to which can be added drugs and fear of crime. With the exception of unemployment and the addition of the infirm elderly, these are also the most acute problems of non-UPAs, but to a far smaller degree. The only problem which is more serious in non-UPAs is the price and quality of public transport. The only problem which appears to have got significantly worse in UPAs is people's health. Of course, to some extent these findings are predictable: UPAs are defined using some of these criteria. But, it seems that with very few exceptions, whatever human problem is taken, it is worse in UPAs and unremittingly so.

2.8   UPA clergy still tend to be slightly younger than non-UPA clergy. A sizeable proportion of all respondents, but particularly those in UPAs, cite personal stress as their most serious problem, followed by personal or family financial problems. Doubts about the worthwhileness of their ministry are expressed by a similar proportion of clergy in both groups. Many – again especially in UPAs – acknowledge difficult relationships with their fellow clergy, church officers and congregation members; however, in this last case, problems seem less widespread than in 1985. Slightly more clergy now depend on family and others for financial support, and more (particularly in non-UPAs) have the burden of caring for dependent relatives.

2.9   Nevertheless, clergy in both UPAs and non-UPAs expressed a high degree of satisfaction in most aspects of their job and overall; this appears if anything to have increased, although the higher degree of satisfaction identified by UPA clergy in the Gallup Poll no longer appears to apply.

2.10   Spouse and family were still the most often-quoted sources of support for male clergy in both UPAs and non-UPAs; there was a heartening increase in the number saying that they received real support from their bishops and senior staff and from their parish officers and congregations.

2.11   Given the fact that the majority of respondents were ordained over ten years ago, it is too soon to observe any effects of changes in initial training patterns – though the reported higher number of ordinands on placement in UPAs than in non-UPAs is encouraging. This tallies with general perceptions that theological colleges and courses now offer such placements, not simply to prepare future clergy for such a ministry, but because engagement with poverty and severe deprivation is seen as an essential part of theological education.

2.12   There appears to have been an increase in the number of both UPA and non-UPA clergy receiving in-service training. Needs identified by a substantial proportion of UPA clergy are training in community work, understanding their surrounding society, fund-raising and management tasks (in the case of the latter, clergy are apparently already receiving more training in this than in any other area apart from spirituality, but still feel that they could do with more).

2.13   In both UPAs and non-UPAs, there appears to be an increase in the tendency for people to join the congregation following a bereavement; many teenagers apparently join through involvement in youth activities. In UPAs it appears that a number of people join congregations through involvement in church-based community projects.

2.14   With regard to the nature of aids to worship, few differences can be observed between UPAs and non-UPAs, apart from the proportionally fewer UPA churches providing the full ASB or prayer book, and the larger number using overhead projectors. This would suggest that liturgical innovation is something being addressed fairly widely in local churches.

2.15   UPA clergy are still more likely than those in non-UPAs to have to meet some of their own personal expenses (indeed the gap has widened) and their parishes face serious financial problems.

2.16   The Gallup survey revealed some dissatisfaction with the state of church buildings, and *Faith in the City* went on to recommend their more imaginative use in UPAs as a community resource, with funding being made available for this purpose (FITC paragraph 7.57). The current survey asked clergy if, over the last ten years, key buildings had been improved, undergone a change of use, or been sold, or still needed improvement The preliminary results suggest a substantial programme of building activity by all churches, but few differences between UPAs and non-UPAs, and a considerable amount of work still needed by both. The only appreciable difference was the greater number of UPA church halls which have undergone improvement or a change of use.

2.17   Nearly all non-UPA parishes and more than half of the UPA parishes appear to have been involved in fund-raising for the Church Urban Fund; more than half of the UPA clergy reported applying for a CUF grant and of these the great majority were successful, at least in part.

2.18   Clergy were asked whether, other than CUF, their churches had collaborated with, and/or received funding from, a list of agencies or programmes in a social or economic regeneration project. UPA clergy reported a total of 35 projects attracting an average of £122,556; among non-UPA clergy, the figures were eight projects and £47,769. By far the largest sources of revenue appear to be local authorities and voluntary organisations, with relatively little coming from central Government and the private sector.

2.19   Many UPA parishes, perhaps two-thirds have undertaken at least one parish audit as recommended in *Faith in the City*; rather fewer non-UPA parishes had done so.

2.20   As with the Gallup survey, respondents were asked to guess the predominant social class of their parish, their congregation and their officers and PCC. In addition, they were asked to give the social class of their parents, to give some indication of their own social origins. Since 1985, the social class distribution of UPA parishes appears to have remained largely unchanged but non-UPA parishes have tended to become more middle class, possibly reflecting general population trends. However, the over-representation of the middle classes in congregations has become even more marked than it was ten years ago. A similar pattern can be discerned in non-UPA congregations. The tendency for PCCs to be disproportionately middle class has likewise become even more marked in both UPA and non-UPA churches. In contrast, the clergy presented a broad mix of social origins, with no significant differences between UPA and non-UPA clergy. These figures would challenge the popular perception of the clergy's uniformly upper middle class origins.

2.21   Fewer than half of the UPA clergy reported that their parishes had a linking-up scheme with a non-UPA parish and in half of those cases it had ceased to operate.

2.22   The final results of the survey and interviews will be reported in due course and will cover in more detail some of the first perceptions identified in this interim report. In addition, it will include material on clergy's hopes and aspirations both personally and for their parishes and, to the extent that the sample permits, on the experiences of women clergy.

Chapter 3

First in the Church

Faith in the City

3.1   When *Faith in the City* was first published ten years ago, it received a mixed reaction in the Church. There were those who watched with nervousness the high profile given to its publication by the press and media; there were those who felt that at last the Church of England was casting off the shackles of its privilege and genuinely siding with the poor and disadvantaged.

3.2   This was a document which did *not* go unnoticed, as do so many Church reports. Sociologists, politicians, clergy and their families, PCCs, house groups, GPs, community workers, business people and unemployed, all reacted to the publication. It is easy to criticise the press and media for unfair reporting of church pronouncements but at least the issues are talked about in pubs, at the school gates, in front of the TV.

> *Can you remember where you lived, what you were doing when* Faith in the City *came out? When did you first hear about it? What did you think or feel?*

3.3   There were 61 recommendations, 38 to the Church, 23 to the nation. The Archbishop's Commission had been as tough on Church policy and practice as it had on the Government and it was important to make sure that the recommendations were taken seriously. The Archbishop of Canterbury appointed an Advisory Group to set the wheels in motion for the implementation of the report. Bishop Tom Butler (then of Willesden) chaired this Group and he was succeeded by Peter Hall, Bishop of Woolwich.

3.4   The Archbishop also appointed an Officer for Urban Priority Areas, the Revd Preb. Pat Dearnley, who was succeeded, in 1989 by the Revd Alan Davis and in 1991 by Gill Moody. Two voluntary honorary assistants, John Chilvers and Geoffrey Brand, each with an area of responsibility and increasing expertise, ensured that the statistical work and the urban policy work were covered in great detail. The Church owes a great deal to these two men; they have given an immense amount of time and effort and are typical of many people across the country who were fired by the vision of *Faith in the City*.

3.5   The Archbishop asked each diocese to appoint a link officer to ensure that the report was debated in diocesan synods, deanery synods and parishes. Out of this came proposals in many dioceses for action. Urban parishes debated the report, recognising the snapshots of their experiences.

3.6   Many other parishes set up groups to study the report with a genuine concern to learn more of conditions in UPAs and to discover how they could respond to the needs of those living in our most deprived areas. Some set up parish links; others felt powerless to do anything until the Church Urban Fund was established and they were offered a clear task, to raise money towards the funding of church-based projects in inner cities.

3.7   In some dioceses link officers became involved in fundraising efforts, in others clear distinctions were made between the need to raise money and the need to give due attention to the many other recommendations in *Faith in the City*. Some worked collaboratively to ensure that the fundraising incorporated elements of education. For instance, in Blackburn, the Bishop of Burnley was chairman of both the *Faith in the City* group and the fundraising group, and the link officer was closely involved with both. A successful pilgrimage to the UPAs of the diocese gave people from other parishes direct experience of areas that they had had no reason to visit in the past. The pilgrimage stressed the notion that a UPA is not a 'Godforsaken' spot, but a place were God is to be found in the experiences and suffering of its people.

3.8   The Church of England's central organisation is complex. The Advisory Group, however, played an important role in bringing the various strands together. The recommendations had been far reaching, covering education, ecumenism, social responsibility, finance and many other areas. As the work proceeded officers from Boards and Councils of Church House were invited to become members of the Group. For many this was the first piece of serious cross-board work they had attempted. Used to working within their own disciplines, officers became aware that their concerns were often shared by others from other Boards. The Advisory Group has always aimed to encourage other Church bodies to take responsibility for particular areas of work, believing that only in this way could *Faith in the City* be said to be in the 'lifeblood of the Church'.

Living Faith in the City

3.9   *Faith in the City* had portrayed the life and environment of those living and worshipping in the deprived inner city areas and outer estates in 1985. The follow-up report *Living Faith in the City* examined the situation four years later, and sought to assess what had been achieved in response to the earlier report and its various recommendations to the Church and nation and to identify what still needed to be done.

3.10   Prominent among the welcome developments in the nation had been the increase in public awareness and concern, which had brought UPAs well to the fore in the political agenda at that time. However, most of the serious human problems identified in the earlier report still remained, and some had actually got worse. The steady improvement in the underlying trend in unemployment was warmly welcomed (although shortly to relapse), but serious regret was expressed at the further sharp widening of the gap between rich and poor which had resulted from taxation and social security policies. Among other areas picked out as of special concern were housing policy and changes in the National Health Service. The former had failed to increase the provision of affordable homes for rent or ownership and had contributed to an increase in homelessness; the latter seemed in danger of creating a two-tier service.

3.11   The response of the Church had been more encouraging, both in parish and diocesan initiatives and in central structures. UPA link officers were active in all dioceses, often with supporting committees. The Church Urban Fund had been set up, diocesan targets to raise £18 million accepted (and two-thirds met) and £5 million so far allocated to over 200 projects in UPAs. Prerequisite to this had been the development of a nationally agreed system for identifying UPA parishes. Some 2000 churches were reported to have undertaken 'parish audits'. The Committee on Black Anglican Concerns had been established, some dioceses had introduced new training initiatives for clergy and laity, and there were reports of significant redeployment of human and financial resources in response to local needs. In recognition of the pressures on clergy, many dioceses had taken steps to reappraise their support systems. Perhaps the big question for the Church was whether the impetus could be maintained and whether its rediscoveries – the concern of the Church as a whole for those in areas of deprivation, the sense of interdependence, and the new vision of hope which had been engendered in so many UPAs – could be sustained and built upon. To this end, the report offered some thoughts on priorities for further action by various parts of the Church.

Ten years on

3.12   In 1992 the House of Bishops assumed direct responsibility for the work, and the Archbishop's Advisory Group became known as the Bishops' Advisory Group. Similarly, the Archbishop's Officer became the Bishops' Officer, reporting annually to the House of Bishops. The Advisory Group is now composed as follows:

- the conveners of link officers in the six regions: they ensure that the concerns of the national network are voiced; they act as a link between the central body and the UPAs themselves

- three General Synod representatives: they make vital links between the Advisory Group and General Synod itself

- officers from the Boards of Education, Social Responsibility, Mission, Ministry and the Committee for Black Anglican Concerns; they bring the experiences of their Boards to the Group and vice versa

- representatives of the Church Urban Fund, the Urban Ecumenical Forum and the Archbishop's Urban Theology Group.

3.13   From 1992 Bishop Tom Butler returned to chair the group and set up an Urban Bishops Panel. This panel is composed of diocesan bishops and suffragans from urban areas who identify growing concerns and issues for wider discussion in the House of Bishops.

3.14   Early in 1995, following a conference entitled 'Faith into Action' which looked at models for church based social action, the Advisory Group agreed Statements of Faith and Intent which set out a framework for its action over the next few years. This is detailed in appendix 1 of this report.

3.15   In addition, it has been asking dioceses and the central Boards to assess their own performance: what have the central Church bodies done since *Faith in the City*? How do they give people in UPAs what they really want and need? What more can they do and when?

Central Boards and Councils

3.16   In 1992 the Advisory Group started asking Boards in turn to answer a series of questions put to them. Boards were asked to make a response to areas of concern identified:

- in the report *Faith in the City* and its follow-up, *Living Faith in the City*

- by link officers either as being currently important in the UPAs in their dioceses or as in some other way important to their task.

3.17   The Group asked that the responses should include;

- guidance as to whether the Board accepts that these concerns are relevant to their terms of reference

- a review as to how far the Board has already addressed these issues

- short and long term proposals for doing so

- proposals for monitoring and evaluating the achievement of objectives identified and for keeping these issues under long-term review.

3.18   But right in the middle of all this, the central Church bodies were suddenly faced with the prospect of making cuts of 10% in their expenditure. Despite this they answered the Advisory Group's questions as positively as they could, but there is no doubt that the bleak realism of the financial situation in the Church has seriously undermined the capacity of central bodies to respond to a range of issues.

3.19   The results of these reviews are summarised in chapter 4 and at the end of each section, BAGUPA has drawn out some particular issues which it believes require further attention.

BAGUPA comment:

3.20   In addition, BAGUPA has two more general points arising from these reviews:

1   In some cases, what the locally based link officers described as 'concerns relevant to a particular Board' were seen by the central body as being 'a matter for the diocese'. The role of diocesan support services is obviously crucial, but so too is that

of central Church bodies. BAGUPA believes that Boards have a clear role in relation to dioceses:

● to provide forums for sharing good practice across dioceses

● to ensure that policies formulated at the centre are informed by local experience and concerns

● to provide guidelines for dioceses on the implementation of centrally agreed policies

● to ensure that in their discussions with other national agencies, including the government, the real experiences and concerns of people are given a voice.

This can only be done through a programme of effective networking, with people skilled at networking in key positions

2   The budgets of central Boards and Councils are extremely modest, even more so in recent years. If Boards are operating in the way described above, they are not simply contributing to an expensive bureaucracy, but fulfilling an essential role. The Church seeks to be active, committed to mission rather than maintenance, but an ill-resourced body is ill-equipped to support such a missionary Church.

Action in dioceses

3.21   Over the years the network of diocesan urban link officers had developed. It had become their responsibility to make sure that dioceses' policies were serving and responding to the experience of the urban Church. This network is still strong, the officers increasingly capable, able to relate to diocesan boards of finance, to local authorities, to people living in the most deprived urban parishes. Link officers in less urban dioceses have attempted to draw the attention of their parishes and diocesan organisations to the nature of the Gospel in UPAs and to the responsibilities of all Christian people to share in their experiences.

> *Who is your urban link officer? Do you know what he/she does in your diocese?*

3.22   At the beginning of 1993 dioceses, following a presentation to the House of Bishops, were sent guidelines on the production of a strategy for UPAs. While recognising the wide variety of dioceses, all at different stages in their planning, it was felt that:

> At times of financial hardship it is even more important for dioceses to develop frameworks against which to make decisions about resources. Against this background the Advisory Group is encouraging dioceses to develop a strategic approach to dealing with their urban priority areas; an approach which both recognises the particular gifts they have to offer the wider Church and their special needs. Dioceses with few urban areas will be encouraged likewise to recognise their responsibility to support the work of churches in urban areas and to be open to their gifts.

3.23   Earlier this year a questionnaire was sent to link officers requesting information on how much had been achieved in terms of diocesan strategy, finance and other related issues. The results are summarised in appendix 2.

BAGUPA comment:

3.24   BAGUPA believes that:

- diocesan Boards should consider how they might develop closer links with their link officer and vice versa, perhaps using the relevant 'Board Review' papers as a basis for discussion

- the move of many dioceses towards developing diocesan strategies is to be commended, and welcomes the commitment of most dioceses to 'quota-by-potential' schemes. It believes, however, that many urban parishes are facing increasing financial difficulties (see chapter 2) and that unless a serious attempt is made to ensure structural support for such parishes, the Church will be failing in its commitment to 'stay in the city'.

Chapter 4

The response of the General Synod Boards and Councils

4.1   As outlined in the previous chapter, central Boards and Councils of the Church of England and others were asked to respond to questions concerning their activities since *Faith in the City* was published. We have attempted to draw out some the most significant material. Unfortunately pressure of space does not permit printing their responses in full, but excerpts are quoted.

Board for Social Responsibility

4.2   The Board for Social Responsibility was the first body to undertake the review. It is clear that there is much overlap between the concerns of the Board and those of the *Faith in the City* network and BAGUPA is grateful to the Board for its co-operation.

4.3   In relation to economic policies, the Board for Social Responsibility accepted its responsibility 'to continue to question the morality of economic policies in the light of their effects'. It pointed to the work of its Industrial and Economic Affairs Committee which seeks to explore the relationship between Christianity and the enterprise culture within a broader context. The stance the Board takes is that 'while acknowledging the central importance of the market, the Board has continued to warn against dogmatic adherence to unregulated market principles'. It has made 'representations to Government on Sunday trading, the ending of the Urban Programme and pit closures, stressing the need for balance – for encouraging the market to operate when it can do so effectively, but always recognising the need for it to operate in a humane context'. It has made a submission to the Commission for Social Justice. The Board identifies taxation as an issue requiring further consideration by Christians, noting how significant an issue it is in determining the political agenda.

4.4   In relation to unemployment, the Board suggests that this 'may be regarded as the single greatest disappointment in the light of *Faith in the City.* The Commission saw employment as a key to unlock many doors. Yet the years since 1985 have seen a rapid growth of fatalism about jobs.' It stresses that it is not a service delivery agency, but accepts a co-ordinating and information-exchange function. It has pursued the issue at European Union level and, with the support of the Industrial and Economic Affairs Committee, an ecumenical initiative, the Churches Enquiry into Unemployment and the Future of Work was launched in September 1995.

4.5   The Board recognises and supports the Industrial Mission networks and Church Action with the Unemployed (now operating within the framework of Church Action on Poverty) in its thinking on these matters.

> Durham: The Churches' Regional Commission is a new body, created after extensive consultation with all denominations across the north east; its remit specifically covers the work of the Churches' ministries of engagement – Industrial Mission, Social Responsibility, Arts and Recreation, Newcastle City Centre Chaplaincy, Teeside's Respond! and urban and rural concerns, to engage purposefully, creatively and strategically with the economic, social and cultural life of the region.

4.6   In relation to community work, the Board has supported the formation of the Churches Community Work Alliance and found external sources of funding. The Alliance has run two national conferences, prepared briefing papers and developed strong regional networks of community workers. As with many other such bodies, this organisation has faced a funding crisis and had to scale down its activities accordingly.

4.7   The recent report on the family, *Something to Celebrate*, prepared by a working party of the Board, placed a strong emphasis on the damaging effects of poverty on family life. Its publication, and the analysis it contained, has been warmly welcomed by many living and working in UPAs, reflecting the reality of life for families struggling to survive and to support one another. The report highlights, too, ways in which the Church can, and indeed does, play an important role in strengthening such families.

4.8   In relation to racial justice, a part-time officer is presently employed whose contribution is maximised by close co-operation with the Churches Commission for Racial Justice, diocesan representatives and secular organisations.

4.9   But what priority does the Board give to UPAs? It suggests that:

● the UPA agenda is always included in the range of possible candidates for new work

● opportunities be taken as they arise to promote UPA concerns, the bulk of the Board's work being responsive by nature

● the Board must encourage an appreciation of the principle of subsidiarity.

4.10   The Board however draws attention to several major difficulties. The first relates to resources:

> The Board sees little value in establishing or maintaining specialist committees or groups without resources. With the loss of its Legal and Criminal Justice post in September 1993, the Board's ability to respond in an important area identified in *Faith in the City* ended.

> In speaking about Church Action with the Unemployed, it points out that the growing financial difficulties facing the Church are posing particular problems for intermediate and ecumenical organisations. This is just one of several areas where the consequences must be noted of the Church Urban Fund's decision to support (almost exclusively) individual projects at the local level. The Fund believed that its aim of putting the Church's money where its mouth was would only have credibility if it supported local projects. Without passing any judgement on that policy, it has to be noted that it left almost completely unfunded (and perhaps unfundable) any so-called intermediate organisations. It also seemed to ignore the experience of Third World charities which shifted their original focus on individual projects to one which sought to support projects which more or less directly contributed to the addressing of 'structural' injustice. It is precisely in this area that ACUPA's success is most questionable. Awareness has been raised, individual projects have done

excellent work but, the critics ask, have causes, mechanisms, and structures of injustice been touched?

4.11   The second relates to Government action. The terms of reference of the BSR require it to promote and co-ordinate the thought and action of the Church in matters affecting the lives of all in society. The Board states that 'in deciding what issues to take up, the Board will ask: is this important and what can we do that others cannot?' It is often easier to accept that an issue is important than to be clear about what a General Synod Board can do about it.'

4.12   In relation to housing for instance, the Board states that it is not a service-delivery organisation, and therefore it cannot build houses or manage housing associations. Nor, the Board states, is it a campaigning organisation: 'The General Synod does not wish it to be a member of the Churches National Housing Coalition.'

4.13   Later in the paper, the Board suggests that, 'the Church is called in the first instance to be a particular kind of community. This may lead it to act with a bias to the poor. It is the Board's task to help the Church to work through the implications of that. It is not the Board's task to do things more appropriately done at diocesan or parish level.'

4.14   Nevertheless, the Board has clearly made regular representations to Government ministers on aspects of policy it considers unjust; it has prepared background papers for General Synod on such topics as housing, community care, debt or the benefits system; opportunities are taken to promote the Board's concerns through debates and questions in the House of Lords, although there is no similar input into the House of Commons.

4.15   However, it notes that many of the recommendations addressed to the Government have been responded to by actions almost diametrically opposed to those called for by *Faith in the City*.

BAGUPA comment:

4.16   **In this summary, BAGUPA has attempted to draw out for Synod some issues of critical importance:**

● **The resourcing of auxiliary Church agencies working in the social field: is this to be left to private individual or corporate charity: should the Church make a corporate contribution: is there a role here for the Church Urban Fund?**

- The resourcing of the BSR itself: is retrenchment of central activities an acceptable long-term strategy for the national Church of an increasingly affluent nation? In the short-term, is the degree of retrenchment in the social field a right expression of priorities?

- Given the present constraint on BSR resources, is the cessation of all work on criminal justice the only possible or the right response?

- The nature of campaigning should be further explored. The high profile given to the publication of *Faith in the City* suggests a clear role for the Church in relation to issues of justice and one which the BSR does, in fact, adopt at times. The Church's actual presence in UPAs, through the parish system, gives it continued authority to speak. More than anything else, this is the factor which causes secular organisations to look to the Church for an authentic voice. The Church's continued commitment to resource this presence, through finance, buildings and personnel provides an example to other bodies. The Church is able to report the harsh realities of the suffering of those in UPAs based on day-to-day experience. Drawing on expertise, prayer and theology, the Church is then in a position to speak with authority and confidence to those in power and to act with justice. This model for campaigning is one which the BAGUPA network has adopted and which it is keen to commend to other Church bodies.

Who in your diocese helps the church to consider issues of social responsibility? How much do they know about what goes on in UPAs? Does your church think about such questions? What do you think of the model of campaigning described above?

Board of Education

4.17   BAGUPA has worked closely with officers of the Board of Education; education is vital in increasing the health and well-being of deprived urban communities.

4.18   It was reassured that 'the Board', its three committees and its officers are all constantly mindful of, and committed to, the thrust of *Faith in the City* and BAGUPA, and that its concerns are indeed relevant to their terms of reference . . . concern for the inner city is now so deeply embedded in our deliberations that disentangling it from our overall work was not an easy task.'

Schools

4.19   In relation to schools, the Board has, through 'advising diocesan directors of education, producing publications and running training courses', affirmed good practice in inner city schools with Christian foundations, affirmed the commitment and work of Christian teachers in UPAs and addressed particular issues which 'arise or have a special focus within schools in inner cities' (e.g. racial violence in schools and society), sought information from BAGUPA and other bodies concerning good practice in UPAs.

4.20   Specifically, the Board recognises that it is part of its function to respond quickly to government initiatives, 'particularly when they are not in the best interest of the schools, pupils and parents in areas of greatest deprivation'. It cites as an example its role in monitoring pilots of the Common Funding Formula, intended to rationalise the funding of grant-maintained and locally managed schools. The Board suggests that 'it is in inner city and rural areas where the operation of the CCF will prove most problematic'.

4.21   In areas of high unemployment, the Board believes that schools have a dual role 'both to encourage pupils to achieve in an environment where good exam results and records of achievement do not bring their reward in terms of employment opportunities; and to create and maintain a school ethos which reflects values which may be difficult to find outside the school gates.'

4.22   In relation to race issues, the Board has run courses focusing on pupils who may have a range of specific needs, including Afro-Caribbean pupils. It also claims that 'by definition good education is anti-racist and this dimension has to be integrated into every aspect of the life of the school'. In addition, 'the educational achievements of black pupils will be higher when they see more black adult role models and when schools feel safer for all pupils – and higher still when teachers' expectations of black pupils reflect their potential'.

4.23   The Board has published guidelines setting out considerations for governing bodies, parents and others discussing moves towards grant-maintained status; among these are two of particular importance. Governors and others are asked to consider 'what are the likely implications of our obtaining grant-maintained status for the other schools in our area and our relationship with them?' and 'what are the likely implications for the LEA of our having grant-maintained status?' It is clearly important in areas of extreme deprivation that no school should be further deprived of adequate resources and support by the break up of local authority provision.

Youth work

4.24   Regarding youth work, the National Youth Officer's job description recognises the need for strategic thinking concerning the Church's work with young people in UPAs. The officer and committee have worked closely with both BAGUPA and the Church Urban Fund helping the CUF to evaluate youth work more effectively and youth officers to advise on preparing good applications. It has effectively acted as a link between the Government and youth officers lobbying the Department of the Environment and Home Office and attracting Government funding. It supports experimental schemes and draws up guidelines for good practice. The particular challenges of youth work in deprived urban areas are well recognised and the Board appears willing to engage with thorny issues such as drugs and crime. The Board points out that field workers have identified possible causes of the increase in the use of drugs; the following have particular relevance for young people in UPAs:

●   poor personal environment and poor personal futures (e.g. housing and unemployment) encouraging the need to escape

●   the growth of drug dealing in a climate of . . . private enterprise by any means necessary which clashes with the collapse of traditional industries and ways of making money.

Teenagers: as a result of a grant from the Church Urban Fund, teenagers on the riot-hit Marsh Farm estate in Luton will this autumn have a range of team sports laid on for the under-occupied teenagers who are marooned there by lack of money and jobs.

Their vicar, Revd John Belither, and members of his congregation will help ex-PE teacher Dave Baxter operate another arm of a scheme already run successfully with 500 teenagers on other estates in the area by Luton Churches Educational Trust.

Work with children

4.25   The Board points to significant developments in work with children. 'The Report *All God's Children* (NS/CHP,1991) challenged local churches to take children seriously and to develop a radical new strategy for children's work and evangelism. The report particularly focused on the nature of society and the way it influences children today. Responding to the findings and recommendations of this report is a major part of the work of the National Officer and diocesan children's advisers.' Officers advise on implementation of the 1988 Children's Act, advise, train and support on request, draw up guidelines for good practice and generally raise the profile of ministry with children, highlighting crucial issues across the whole Church. Despite this, the Board points out that 'UPAs have not been given a particular priority over other areas. Advisers do not have the financial resources to stimulate new work or specific projects in UPAs such as the exciting work mentioned in the Summer 1994 edition of the Church Urban Fund's newsletter *Faith and Action* which highlights areas of work where children's needs are being met through CUF grants.'

4.26   The Board states that 'commitment to ministry with children in UPAs and the issues that surround that ministry, is a concern of the National Officer and diocesan advisers but is not seen as a priority over and above work in other areas'.

Further and higher education

4.27   Of particular interest in the field of further education are the Board's collaborative efforts in dioceses which include:

the promotion of closer links between parish incumbents and staff with their local FE sector college, in particular raising awareness of college provision for guidance, education and training services for the unemployed, the disadvantaged, the minority groups, and those with special needs, the encouraging of local church collaboration with colleges in matters relating to the provision of short courses and training for redundant workers and unemployed school leavers and the supporting of parish initiatives like the Anglican Patchwork Graphics Communications Projects in Leeds.

4.28   Trends in higher education have caused an expansion of the system:

Indeed, there are now more mature student entrants to higher education than 18 year old school leavers. Inevitably, some have come from those previously untapped socio-economic groups living in UPAs. Not only do these new entrants swell the number engaged in HE, they also bring a welcome change of ethos to a system which previously supported economic, social and political privilege for a small section of society.

4.29   The Board draws attention to growing financial hardship among students and the key role chaplains have to play in drawing attention to this and in referring students to appropriate sources of hardship funds, although this is no substitute for adequate levels of funding.

4.30   Chaplains, too, are able to bridge the gap between the institutions and their local community. Many institutions of higher education are located in or near UPAs, including a large percentage of new universities which were formally polytechnics. Of particular interest is an initiative undertaken at Wolverhampton where 'Church Studies' is undertaken as part of the curriculum, a course which offers particular opportunities for links with local people forged by the chaplain.

4.31   In addition, some of the Church colleges of higher education, supported by the Board and the National Society, established the Urban

Learning Foundation which introduces teachers in training and others to aspects of education in an urban environment.

Adult education

4.32   In many dioceses adult education advisers work closely with CME officers to encourage the establishment of lay leadership programmes. The Board points to the enormous potential, especially in UPAs 'for opening up access to opportunities for work or further training by concentrating on demonstration of competency rather than examination'.

> In London's Docklands, at St Peter's, Wapping, an old school building has been developed into a community education centre. Special adult interest groups are operated there and younger visitors are helped over access to training. There is also a permanent job club to tutor people seeking work. The aim of the centre, which has had five grants from the Church Urban Fund since 1989, is to encourage the development of the community for which it is now a focus – not only for education, but for social gatherings and the arts.

4.33   In particular relation to UPAs, the purpose of adult education is described as:

> to work with those in UPAs to develop confidence and skill so that they can have a voice in the present Church structures and so that they can go on and challenge the structures, working with their agendas to open up possibilities especially through team and community action.

4.34   The Board has encouraged everyone to be more aware of the needs of people with little or no desire to read by improving the accessibility of their written work and by the use of cassettes, videos and popular culture, including films.

4.35   The Board works closely with the National Institute of Adult and Continuing Education, through which 'it has been possible to contest

Government policy when it is perceived to be threatening non-academic and informal adult education, which is where many people with painful memories of school days may be tempted to start again.'

BAGUPA comment:

4.36　BAGUPA is particularly grateful to the Board of Education for the detailed response to its questions. It is aware of the vital role played by Church schools in UPAs and commends in addition any initiatives which recognise the often close involvement between parishes and LEA or grant-maintained schools. BAGUPA's main concern is the apparent lack of priority accorded to UPAs in its children's work. Acknowledging the limited resources of the Board, it questions whether more might be done to recognise the particular needs of disadvantaged children. The Board, in this context, acknowledges the imaginative work taking place in Church Urban Funded projects and there is an argument for closer working between the CUF and the Children's Work Committee (see the Youth Committee's response) to ensure that this work has maximum benefit to the whole Church. BAGUPA looks forward to further discussion about potential areas of development.

> *Inside and outside your congregation, how might education be used to empower those who are less powerful than others? Do you have contacts with your local schools? To what extent is your diocesan Board of Education aware of the issues outlined here?*

Advisory Board of Ministry

4.37　The Advisory Board of Ministry has a broad remit which covers many areas of direct concern to urban priority areas. Selection and training, patterns of ministry and deployment, are matters which ultimately affect the leadership offered to congregations in urban areas.

4.38　In the introduction to the paper ABM made a number of general points:

There is a proper tension between the central bodies of the Church of England and individual dioceses. This is particularly apparent in matters of ministry where there is a desire for local initiative, identification of appropriate ministries to suit local needs, differing strengths and resources in different parts of the country. This is held over against a desire for the sharing between different regions and dioceses of human and material resources, consistency of quality particularly in relation to the ordained ministry, and appropriate structures to ensure that these necessary tensions are held in balance. These are issues which are being addressed by the Turnbull Commission.

4.39   ABM 'seeks to be constantly aware of issues in relation to ministry in UPA areas as it also holds before itself issues in relation to rural ministry, ministry by members of ethnic minorities and the need for close co-operation with ecumenical partners. ABM seeks to consult and to listen to the voices of all sectors of the Church.'

4.40   In addition, 'within the present structures there are constraints of finance and human resources. The current need to identify a 10% reduction is going to affect work in Vocations, CME and Ministry among Deaf People.'

Selection and initial training

4.41   In relation to selection, ABM points out that a working party has undertaken a thorough investigation into the procedures for selection and this working party has consulted with the Bishops' Officer; it has clearly attempted to take seriously the need to value candidates from disadvantaged backgrounds and BAGUPA awaits the results to see to what extent this is achieved. The report was accepted by ABM and then by the House of Bishops in June 1995. It was published as *Review of Selection Procedures* in September 1995, ABM Policy Paper No. 6. The new procedures will be implemented in January 1997.

4.42   Vocation work 'is carried on in conjunction with dioceses' vocations advisers and in co-operation with other areas, e.g. stewardship, to promote vocations to Christian ministry of all sorts. Student vocation conferences held in 1994 and 1995 entitled 'Hope in the City' have been looking at ministry in UPA parishes. These courses were based at the Royal Foundation of St Katharine in Stepney.

4.43   Recent shifts in initial training now provide for a more flexible approach, with part-time and non-residential courses available to prepare for both stipendiary and non-stipendiary ministry.

4.44   The content of such training still varies considerably from institution to institution. ABM states that:

> In line with the recommendations of Occasional Paper No.29, colleges' and courses' plans for urban study centres and attachments are now submitted to ABM as part of the institution's overall submission under ACCM 22. In the same way the ABM Finance Committee seeks guidance on institutions' plans in this area. Many colleges have attachments to urban centres which include a substantial continuous period of full-time residence. In general, the recommendations of that report have been followed.

4.45   ABM was asked by BAGUPA: what weight is given when advising and evaluating the training programmes of theological colleges and courses to:

- understanding the social context of UPAs

- the need to organise personal workloads and to plan effectively

- an understanding of ministry in relation to mission and social responsibility

- an understanding of ministry in a multi-faith environment

- sharing and leading ministry

- racism awareness and equal opportunities

4.46   The Board responded that 'the issues in this section are widely focused on the colleges' and courses' exploration of ministry in particular settings, many of which are UPA. Particular issues in this list have been the focus of pastoral studies' units especially relating ministry to mission and social responsibility, ministry in a multi-faith environment and racism awareness and equal opportunities.'

4.47   ABM has responded to *Faith in the City* in respect of racism and the development of vocations amongst black people in a number of ways, including major involvement in the foundation of the Simon of Cyrene Theological Institute and in promoting, in 1993, a conference of those involved in theological education 'Facing the Challenge of Racism'. The papers of this consultation are published by ABM with the Runnymede Trust as *ABM Ministry Paper No.8.*

Continuing ministerial education

4.48   Continuing ministerial education has a vital role to play in enabling existing clergy to assimilate and explore the insights of urban ministry. A growing proportion of clergy have experience of such ministry which they have found challenging and often extremely rewarding. The ABM officer responsible for CME sent a detailed questionnaire to dioceses to attempt to glean what CME is available, and what induction and debriefing procedures in relation to UPA ministry are provided by dioceses. BAGUPA is grateful for the energy expended on this. Twenty-nine dioceses replied, of which nineteen were very informative.

4.49   In relation to induction courses 'a few dioceses indicated CME courses designed specifically for UPA and urban ministry. These tended to be the larger dioceses with substantial urban populations. These included courses on doing urban theology, urban social issues, ministry among ethnic minorities and ministry on outer estates.' The majority, however, offer generalised courses for clergy starting a new incumbency or taking up a new post. These are designed 'to be applicable regardless of the context of the ministry being taken up'. No diocese indicated any debriefing process for clergy leaving UPA ministry for a non-urban post.

4.50   'The overall picture is of good general provision in terms of induction and other ministry skills courses, but with varied provision of specific UPA courses. Those dioceses with few UPA parishes or limited resources particularly lacked these. This may well be another instance of where dioceses should be encouraged to work together. This would have to be based on a clear understanding of the actual training needs and of how they are best addressed, including an identification of current resources.' Several external agencies and resources were listed specifically by respondents, namely, the Childrens' Society, Selly Oak Colleges, the Sheffield Urban Theology Unit, Urban Ministry Fellowship and the Committee for Black Anglican Concerns.

4.51   In CME, 'UPA ministry is one specific form of ministry among several for which particular training requests are made. Indeed, a number of replies from the CME officers asked why the questions were not directed to rural ministry. The standard practice has been, therefore, to provide general induction and skills courses, as indicated above, applicable to a wide range of ministries. Specialised provision is the supplementary to this general programme. Questions remain about the effectiveness, on the one hand, and feasibility on the other, of general or specialised courses.'

> The Revd Peter Jones is a community priest, without a church building, exploring patterns of community ministry through a CUF project which supports initiatives on health, education and training in South Devonport.

Patterns of ministry

4.52   At the end of 1994 local non-stipendiary ministry schemes were operating in seven dioceses, with seven other schemes in preparation. A thorough review of LNSM will be undertaken starting in 1995 and BAGUPA looks forward to participating in this review to assess the value or otherwise of such schemes for urban priority areas.

4.53   Lay ministry does not at present fall strictly within the remit of ABM, although there is growing co-operation between ABM and the Board of Education with the Board of Mission in keeping in touch with developments in lay ministry in dioceses.

Deployment

4.54   ABM has been asked to advise the House of Bishops about the revision or replacement of the Sheffield and other formulae for clergy deployment to meet the current situation. It did not, however, spell out to what extent these take into account social factors. ABM also pointed out that 'the distribution of clergy within dioceses is a proper responsibility of the bishop and those who advise him'. It is far from clear whether guidelines are offered to assist dioceses in such decisions, whether by ABM or the House of Bishops or any other body.

BAGUPA comment:

4.55   BAGUPA is grateful to ABM for its submission, but it believes that this response raises some significant questions for the Church.

4.56   The first relates to the prioritisation of UPAs. ABM's response could be interpreted as suggesting that UPAs are one among many interest groups pressing for time in competition with other equally vocal bodies. In some respects this may be true, but this highlights that basic question: in what sense are people living in places of extreme deprivation accorded a priority within the life of the Church?

4.57   Most clergy who have experienced UPA ministry describe its powerful formative influence on their development. Direct engagement with poverty sharpens up a Gospel often clouded in other areas by self-interest and comfort. The unshrouded Gospel of Christ's passion and resurrection is daily lived out in the experiences of people living in extreme poverty. This, in summary, is at the heart of the priority which the Church should be according to urban priority areas; a priority which recognises the value of UPAs to the whole Church itself and which directs resources to that end. Are UPAs viewed as interest groups or a living expression of Christ's presence with humankind?

4.58   BAGUPA's second point relates to resources and terms of reference. ABM has been severely tested over recent years. In its lap has fallen a whole range of issues. In addition, it has dealt as always with selection, training, ministerial development and vocation: how much of the work it does concerns ministry itself; how much is concerned with basic questions of employment practice? This has been exacerbated by 10% cuts. BAGUPA questions whether ABM has the capacity or resources at present to undertake long-term thinking about UPA ministry whilst it has such a heavy workload. For instance, BAGUPA suggests that induction and debriefing procedures for UPA clergy should be a priority if valuable time in post is not to be wasted. At present most clergy take several months (years even) discovering some very basic skills and insights which might otherwise have been gained from a short induction process. Similarly, who harvests the rich experiences of UPA clergy before they leave to take up another post? Who helps them to evaluate what they have learned or listens to their, often considerable, guilt about leaving? Yet central support for CME is to be cut to a quarter-time post. CME might be the responsibility of each diocese, but who will ensure that such schemes are researched and promoted?

4.59   ABM has a responsibility for the accreditation of some forms of lay ministry. The Board of Education also has a role in advising on modular systems of training for those wishing to develop skills in ministry. The two Boards work closely together but neither is authorised or resourced to take overall responsibility for promoting theological reflection on the nature of lay ministry or for looking at employment practice in relation to paid, but unaccredited, lay workers. Many churches currently employ such workers; over 250 of these are partly funded by the Church Urban Fund and most are on short-term contracts. Many more people in UPA congregations are working in a voluntary capacity in church-based community projects. Yet insufficient thought has been given to how this development informs an understanding of ministry. BAGUPA suggests that a secure location for such work must be a priority.

4.60   Finally, in relation to deployment of clergy it must be helpful to a diocese to have the perspective of the national pattern and inter-diocesan comparisons against which to exercise its deployment responsibility - especially in relation to UPAs of which some dioceses have little experience. Who, other than ABM, is in a position to provide an overview and a forum for sharing experience, or to draw attention to the sort of deployment statistics shown in appendix 4?

Who in your diocese helps people to discover their own sense of ministry? Do you encourage those who are less confident or new to the church to feel that their ministry is valued? What might be the particular pressures on those in positions of ministerial leadership in UPAs? Does your vicar have experience of UPA ministry which he or she could share with you?

Central Board of Finance

4.61   BAGUPA has had strong links with the CBF, partly through the statistical work of John Chilvers which has required close liaison between the two departments. This has been strengthened by the decision of the CBF Statistics Department to accept responsibility for the administration and upkeep of the new Index of Deprivation based on 1991 census figures.

Financing the work of Synod

4.62   The CBF states that 'the formulation of the annual budget by the CBF is informed by the Policy Committee and by the priorities identified by Boards and Councils in their annual budget plans, where these are consistent with the overall priorities set by the Policy Committee. However the CBF has to ensure that the budget is formed within the total forecast of expenditure which the dioceses are likely to support.' Specifically, the CBF would be prepared to discuss with Boards and Councils the particular budgetary provision for their support to UPAs when considering with them their draft budget submission.

Christian stewardship

4.63   The Stewardship Committee agreed that there 'is anecdotal evidence supported by some statistical information that giving in some UPA parishes is proportionately higher than in other areas. Giving may be proportionately higher because:

●   there is more evidence of the need, which inspires greater generosity from those who are actively involved

●   the method of apportioning quota may appear in some cases to have a disproportionately adverse affect on UPAs

●   the congregation may be eclectic and not reflect the economic nature of the parish

●   we know from the teaching of Jesus that the possession of wealth can inhibit a faithful response to calls for generosity. There is evidence that those in poorer circumstances respond proportionately with greater generosity to such a call.'

4.64   One significant question for the Stewardship Department related to the effect on stewardship of a growing understanding of community ministry, with unclear boundaries between the congregation and the wider community. In response to this the committee pointed to the report *Of Your Own* which 'acknowledged that Christian Stewardship is about the discovery and use of human material and spiritual resources to their best effect. . . The department has not tackled this issue with particular reference to UPAs because its major preoccupation is the fundamental teaching of discipleship to the whole Church.'

4.65   Importantly, in response to a question about presenting the case for interdependence, the CBF pointed out that stewardship 'guards against congregationalism and encourages individuals and parishes to support one another through interdependence. Systems that apportion diocesan costs so that the strong support the weak are to be encouraged and with the reduced ability of the Church Commissioners to help the poorer dioceses, the Church does need a mechanism to ensure that appropriate help crosses diocesan boundaries.'

4.66   In September 1993 two quota conferences were held to provide an opportunity for dioceses to learn of the methods and experiences of others. 'There was clearly a wide spectrum of views, and no attempt was made to identify an ideal system which was described at the workshop as "the one which works best for you!"' A report was issued. These ideas were explored further by the Bishops' Officer for UPAs in an article produced for *Full Measure*, the journal of the Anglican Stewardship Association in May 1995. This is reproduced in appendix 3.

Statistics department

4.67   The core work of the CBF statistics department is the collection and processing of finance and membership statistics from the parishes, the main purpose of which is to provide a foundation on which various central apportionment and allocation systems can be based.

4.68   In addition, the department undertakes work at the request of other central Church organisations. It takes some initiatives of its own; the department is planning, for instance, a 'one-off' enquiry of parishes, co-incident with the routine annual returns, to elicit information in areas of Church life where statistics are scarce at present .

4.69   'Nevertheless', the Board points out, 'it remains that there is no overarching body which has sole or ultimate responsibility for ensuring the provision of statistics with the general aim of informing the Church of England as a whole. One obvious consequence of this is that there is no obvious mechanism by which statistical priorities can be evaluated. For instance, if the demand for slots in the proposed questionnaire to parishes is too great.'

4.70   BAGUPA's questions to the Board concerning statistics should be seen in the light of this last statement. Increasingly those in UPAs working alongside local authorities and other agencies are aware of the value of using information available from the Census and other sources to define more clearly the task of the Church in such areas. The compilation of the Index of Deprivation is one such example. The CBF presently only uses such data as a means of converting a limited number of other official statistics from county or district to a diocesan base (e.g. personal incomes, unemployment ratios, where relevant to diocesan contributions to Synod's budget, or to the Church Commissioners allocations). However, in tandem with the Commissioners, the CBF is looking at the possibility of using the Index as a measure of diocesan deprivation, with possible applications to allocations and General Synod apportionment. The CBF statistics department does not presently have the remit or the capacity to do what BAGUPA asked, namely 'use census data and other official statistics (e.g. area health) to ensure that the Church of England has understood the society it serves'.

4.71   BAGUPA also asked about the availability of statistics in user-friendly form for parishes and dioceses. The Church Statistics booklet has recently begun to incorporate graphical representations, but generally information is supplied (particularly to *ad hoc* requests) in the form of tables and spreadsheets.

Investment management

4.72   The CBF endeavours to operate a clear but sensible ethical policy, with a regard to both negative and positive considerations. In this context, BAGUPA asked 'what positive strategies might be adopted to encourage companies to create jobs in UPAs'.

4.73   In response the CBF stated that 'its Investment Office has regular contact with companies in which it invests and has therefore the opportunity to raise the subject of UPAs with its management. It cannot of course advocate policies that are not in the interests of the company's shareholders but it can encourage management to consider the creation of jobs in UPAs where possible and seek their views on the possibilities of doing so. In addition, it can also focus on companies that donate to community projects, second staff to provide business expertise and otherwise play a social role in their local communities.'

4.74   'The Investment Management Committee will monitor this matter by arranging for the CBF Funds to report to it periodically about the responses which it has received from companies.'

The Central Church Fund

4.75   The Central Church Fund has been supportive of many local initiatives in UPAs. Its criteria are broad and often of significance to deprived urban areas which might not be eligible for a grant from the Church Urban Fund (for instance, initiatives intended to meet the needs of people living in small pockets of deprivation which are not UPAs).

BAGUPA comment:

4.76   BAGUPA is grateful to the CBF for the care taken over making its submission. In addition, it was one of the few bodies prepared to commit itself on paper to specific new initiatives on behalf of UPAs. BAGUPA has concerns about the weight attached by the Stewardship Committee to the committed congregation as the source of gifts; this it considers to be contrary to the thrust of much work in UPAs since *Faith in the City*. CBF's emphasis on inter-dependence is welcomed. BAGUPA feels strongly that, both centrally (between dioceses) and within them (between parishes), the mechanism should be in the form of an equitably shared financial burden rather than a system of hand-outs. BAGUPA also calls for the development of a central statistics department to provide the sort of information and social analysis needed by dioceses and parishes; this to be tied in much more closely with clearly identified and centrally agreed priorities.

4.77   Despite these concerns, BAGUPA welcomed the work of the Board in pursuing equal opportunities in Church House and in organising the recent quota conferences, which are to be repeated in 1996. The positive tone of the Investment Committee was particularly welcome. In addition, the Statistics Department has recently taken over the administration and upkeep of the new Index of Deprivation. Most importantly, the Board points to a method of ensuring ongoing prioritisation for UPAs in the future. Whatever structures are put in place following the report of the Turnbull Commission, prioritisation by the Policy Committee, followed by implementation through the budgeting processes could have a significant impact on the support offered by Boards and Councils to UPAs.

> *Who holds the purse strings in your parish and diocese? Is room made and training offered for those from less affluent backgrounds to participate in financial decisions? Does your Diocesan Board of Finance know of the pressures on UPA congregations? Does it know the relative levels of giving per member (or pledged giver) in UPAs and non-UPAs? Are differences between them reasonable? Does it have investment policies which support the creation of jobs and other financial opportunities in UPAs or other deprived areas? Does your stewardship programme recognise people from outside the congregation as a resource? Should it?*

Church Commissioners

4.78   The Church Commissioners have been supportive of the work of BAGUPA and the Church Urban Fund, offering where possible staff time and other assistance, particularly in the development of the new Index of Deprivation. They provided detailed responses to the BAGUPA review, which are here summarised.

Historic resources

4.79   When referred back to an original recommendation in *Faith in the City* concerning the redistribution of historic resources, they responded as follows:

4.80   *Faith in the City* envisaged the possible redistribution of all or part of the Commissioners' perpetuity allocations to dioceses. Policy in the late 80s was to allow 'perpetuity' allocations to continue unaltered but to target new money on to the neediest dioceses as a means of 'levelling up' the historic resources of the neediest dioceses. The formula for targeting this money was 50% weighted towards historic resource income per Sheffield man, 25% to 'potential' per Sheffield man (calculated on the basis of Church membership and average earnings) and 25% in respect of unemployment levels (which at that time diverged quite widely). This policy made significant strides in levelling the resources backing stipends etc.; by the early 90s some of the poorest dioceses had the highest levels of historic resources when the Commissioners allocations were taken into account.

4.81 The availability of the Parsonages Renewal Fund between 1986 and 1990 on a selective basis also helped those predominantly northern dioceses who lacked sufficient capital resources to fund new projects.

4.82 For the last few years the focus has changed from increasing discretionary allocations to cutting them back in order to reduce over-distribution (which is eroding capital). This has been done in a way which has so far borne most heavily on the richer dioceses, most of which stand to lose most or all of their allocations (including 'perpetuity' allocations) by 1996. We have done this by reducing the allocations on a half flat-rate (i.e. £x per minister) and half selective approach (with the same formula as described above). This has been combined with cuts in other expenditure in order to maintain allocations as high as possible: for example, the overall cut in diocesan support in 1995 is £12 million, but only £3 million of this has been routed through allocations.

4.83 However, the scale of over-distribution is such that we cannot avoid further and deeper cuts, and here we face a real dilemma because, as the richer dioceses fall out of the picture, the effect of further cuts becomes concentrated on the 'neither rich nor poor' dioceses and finally the neediest dioceses. We are currently exploring with dioceses whether there is any way in which we can provide better protection to the neediest dioceses (e.g. by asking dioceses to re-imburse us for certain categories of statutory expenditure).

4.84 In addition, the Commissioners say that while 'actual giving' is analysed by the CBF and is not part of the existing allocation formula, they are investigating the possibility of protecting ministry in deprived urban areas by:

● laying more emphasis on the relativities of potential giving

● including an assessment of local deprivation (probably Oxlip).

Funding of pensions

4.85   The Commissioners state that they are 'committed to resolving the pensions issue in such a way as to leave an adequate support fund for the poorer parishes and dioceses. This is a high priority.'

4.86   In addition, 'the principle of interdependence is coming to the fore in our discussions about the future funding of pensions. We have illustrated to dioceses the choices to be made on how the funding responsibilities are split between the Commissioners and dioceses, and the possible consequences of those choices for the Commissioners' allocations capacity. We believe dioceses are largely supportive of the Commissioners' concern to ensure that capacity is adequate and that dioceses recognise a moral responsibility to ensure that funding arrangements recognise the principle of interdependence.'

Sale of redundant churches

4.87   *Faith in the City* recommended that 'in cases of the sale of redundant churches there should be earlier and more open consultation with community organisations and bodies such as Housing Associations when future uses are being considered' (paragraph 7.57).

4.88   In response the Commissioners suggest that 'community and housing uses are one of the most favoured group of uses for redundant churches, although development control and listed building considerations present difficulties in some cases. . . Up to the end of 1993, out of 771 redundant churches put to alternative use, 188 had been appropriated to civic, cultural or community purposes, 11 had been sold to housing associations and 1 to a local authority for residential conversion. In the same period, out of 313 redundant churches appropriated to demolition and site disposal, 59 sites of demolished churches had been sold to housing associations and 47 to local authorities.'

4.89   'The Commissioners will continue to encourage dioceses to pursue such uses.'

4.90   Regarding consultation, the Commissioners suggest that 'the local community is always brought in when notices about proposed schemes are published and also served on the local planning authority'.

4.91   The long-drawn out process for declaration of redundancy can contribute to the wider environmental neglect obvious in many UPAs.

The Commissioners do take a pro-active role in trying to ensure that the future of redundant churches is settled within the three-year waiting period and earlier if possible. They have also established performance targets to ensure that proposals for redundancy are dealt with swiftly.

4.92   In relation to the use of redundant church buildings by other faiths:

> the guidance given is such that the use of (redundant) church buildings is not to be regarded as an evidently suitable use which a diocesan committee should seek or prefer to other types of use. If nevertheless, a case arises where the committee, with the support of the bishop, wish the Commissioners to consider such a proposal, then the Commissioners judge the suitability of the proposed use on its merits taking into account all the relevant circumstances, such as:
>
> - the beliefs, practices and attitudes to the Christian Church of the particular non-Christian body
>
> - the historic and architectural nature and importance of the redundant building; the effect of any structural alterations needed to facilitate the proposed use; and the general significance of the building in the local and wider Christian community
>
> - the availability of other alternative uses for the redundant building, especially by another Christian denomination
>
> - the views of the local Anglican congregation and other Christian and representative figures.
>
> There is no intention at present to review this policy.

Support for the Church Urban Fund

4.93   The Commissioners express hope that 'in the longer term there may be scope to make further allocations to CUF whose work we continue to support through a 'gift in kind' (worth some £0.25 million p.a), but all our policies are subject to review in the light of our long-term financial projections of likely resources and liabilities.'

Glebe Sales

4.94   Despite the need to obtain the best possible deal reasonably attainable, the Commissioners state that 'opportunities do arise which allow glebe sales for affordable housing or community purposes' and that 'several such schemes have gone ahead with the active approval of the Commissioners'.

Other points

4.95   In relation to:

- rents on the Commissioners estates: the Commissioners say 'that they have a moral obligation and a legal requirement to produce a proper return on their assets'. In most instances this involves looking for market rents on most of their agricultural, commercial and residential estates, with the exception of the Octavia Hill Estates, where 'reasonable rents' are set at levels which go most but not all of the way towards market rents. Individual cases of genuine financial hardship are treated sympathetically

- communications: the Commissioners are reviewing the format of their publications to make them more user-friendly in a local context and continue to make presentations directly to parishes;

- digitisation of parish maps: the Commissioners have explored this idea but at present the costs are prohibitive.

BAGUPA comment:

4.96   BAGUPA is grateful to the Commissioners for ongoing dialogue, particularly in relation to the future financing of ministry in UPAs. It believes that this issue is critical if the Church of England is to maintain its presence in areas where many other organisations have withdrawn.

4.97   BAGUPA calls for a system of financing ministry in UPAs which:

- minimises the financial burden on congregations there

- allows for financial stability to assist long term planning. Any system of making allocations on a parochial base must not rely on a process of bidding from year to year. Those involved in voluntary organisations and Church Urban Funded projects will be aware of the harsh realities of short-term funding arrangements

● reinforces the principle of interdependence, whether between parishes or dioceses.

4.98 BAGUPA suggests the organisation of a consultation involving UPA link officers, ACORA officers, chairmen and secretaries of the DBFs, Commissioners, CBF staff and others in order to work toward some realistic methods of financing ministry in UPAs and other deprived areas.

4.99 BAGUPA very much hopes that cash allocations to the Church Urban Fund are resumed as soon as possible.

How are parishes and people in your diocese encouraged to recognise the principle of an inter-dependent church?

Board of Mission

4.100 BAGUPA has worked closely with officers of this Board and is grateful for the very full response to its questions. In its introduction the Board claims that 'urban conditions, urban life, ministry and theology have much to teach us and to contribute to our overall understanding of mission. Therefore we like to think that *Faith in the City* and *Living Faith in the City* are directly relevant to our work, but we are seeking to go beyond what is said in these, to integrate our learning and understanding in ways which will enhance the whole Church. In a decade of evangelism we see this as particularly crucial.'

London is seeing a new challenge to churches to recognise the value of project work in enabling a deepening of discipleship among the users and organisers of the projects. 'Apt liturgies' make the connection between people's real concerns and the Christian faith (e.g. a debt project organised a first birthday service on the theme of debt.

Evangelism

4.101   John Finney, the Board's former National Officer for Evangelism, produced research in *Finding Faith Today* which reveals how people come to faith through a process rather than through a crisis approach. The Board's emphasis therefore is on 'building missionary congregations' rather than on campaigns.

4.102   The present National Officer for Evangelism points out that even 'if the appropriate pattern for UPA evangelism is where evangelism and social action are united, e.g. thrift shops. . . if the appropriate spirituality is not present, nothing will get through them.' In his book *Being Human, Being Church*, he continues to look at spirituality and mission in the local church. The Board of Mission is also interested in the kind of mission audit which looks at the constituent features of a parish (shops/schools/launderettes) and the geographical landmarks of the people, churched and unchurched, to see how these might be matched for process evangelism.

4.103   The Decade Office is aware of the importance of appropriate forms of worship for those from a non-book culture, and of the need to share examples of good practice in evangelism in UPAs.

Appropriate models of mission for urban areas

4.104   The forthcoming document *A Time for Sharing* looks at:

> the concept of Church centres as being particularly appropriate to mission in urban areas. These Church centres may be based in Church buildings, but be staffed by professionals unconnected with the Church, such as social workers, drug counsellors, financial advisers. Here people may become familiar with the Church environment and find it easier to respond to invitations to join with others in Church events such as mothers and toddlers or a lunch club. One offshoot of such a process is exemplified in a second-hand clothes shop run by Church members which is not overtly evangelistic, but which offers an invitation to customers to a coffee evening which customers will know is overtly evangelistic.

4.105   Church planting in under-churched areas was recently explored in the document *Breaking New Ground*. This may have particular relevance to parishes which include large estates where the Church has not previously been able to make inroads.

4.106 The National Officer for Evangelism sees outreach through pastoral ministry leading inevitably towards social justice and the confrontation of unjust structures.

Mission and culture

4.107 There is ongoing work relating the Gospel to popular culture, which has particular relevance for UPAs. In particular, the Theology Secretary has produced work on the *Gospel as Public Truth for London* which includes an evaluation of life in the inner city in the context of the Church's public role. The diocesan missioners have looked at the theological implications of the question 'Is there a Gospel for the rich?' seeking to relate this to urban mission.

Mission from Urban Priority Areas to the wider Church

4.108 Some work has been done by the Theology Secretary on matching stories from England illustrating the Anglican Consultative Council's five marks of mission (including material from the Church Urban Fund's publication *Stories of Hope*) with similar stories from overseas. It is hoped that these might form part of a World Mission Audit pack.

4.109 The Mission in England Committee, in addition, has supported visits to UPAs for participants to reflect theologically on what is happening in Church life there.

4.110 In earlier discussions with ACUPA and then BAGUPA the Board says that they 'have heard that earlier experiments on linkage' (between UPA and non-UPA parishes) 'were not normally very successful and that the difficulties outweighed the gains. We have therefore not pursued this as a Board.' Despite this the Board recognises that local, informal experiments and linkages are still taking place.

Inter-faith issues

4.111 The Board has an Inter-faith Consultative Group which is well aware that for 'many inner city residents, their faith is the most significant way in which they define their identity and culture'. The staff member responsible was a member of the planning group for BAGUPA's conference on Faith, Race and Culture in 1993.

4.112   The Board points, in addition, to the Bradford diocese strategy document on inter-faith relations produced in 1992 and the draft pastoral regulations on inter-faith issues produced by Chelmsford diocese. (The adviser for the latter runs the Manor Park Faith in Community Project in East London).

> The Curry Project is a collaborative enterprise organised by representatives of a variety of faith communities in the Bradford diocese. Groups include the Moslem Eid Committee, the Bradford Sikh Temples, Hindu Street Kids, the Anglican chaplaincy, local Roman Catholics and Methodists, staff and students from the local college and university. Its aim is to provide good quality evening meals in warm and pleasant surroundings, the chance to chat, receive welfare advice and be referred to emergency accommodation. The project is hoping to expand so that clientele will take a more active part in food preparation, learning basic catering skills. Smaller, more committed support groups are planned, drawn from the present clients and staff.

Rural affairs

4.113   The Rural Affairs Sub-committee has a remit wider than rural mission and 'although it appears on the surface to be least likely to engage with urban issues, the staff member has been seeking to learn from the indices of deprivation and would like to consider similarly an index for rural deprivation'. From the new Oxlip Index, the prediction of numbers dependent on low incomes should prove as informative to rural parishes as to UPAs; and the other Census data, to which all dioceses are offered access through the computer programme related to the Index, should be equally helpful to parishes in all types of areas.

BAGUPA comment:

4.114 BAGUPA will continue to work closely with the Board on several initiatives described above. It regrets the apparent failure of so many attempts to link UPA and non-UPA parishes, but believes that, when resources permit, it would be worth the Board exploring those initiatives which have been productive, to discover what factors are important in strengthening the bond. Much of the Board's work on missionary congregations ties in closely with insights beginning to emerge from the action of many congregations in UPAs. The development of mission audits provides an opportunity to carry forward the original recommendation in *Faith in the City* that parishes prepare parish audits. BAGUPA will continue to liaise closely with the Board in this area.

4.115 BAGUPA also feels that it should have a much closer relationship with the Rural Affairs Committee, dealing as they both do with issues of poverty and deprivation. This could be particularly important in the next few years as the Church attempts to define a method for maintaining financial interdependence across dioceses.

> *Has your parish completed a mission audit or a parish audit? Were these different? Do they need up-dating? Do you think that mission involves social action in the community?*

Council for Christian Unity

4.116 The Council is to foster ecumenical work in the Church nationally and in the dioceses and to promote unity and ecumenical concerns in the work of all Boards and Councils of the General Synod. In its work with Boards and Councils it seeks to work in a very similar way to BAGUPA. Indeed, the Council has recently carried out a series of reviews similar to that undertaken by BAGUPA.

Local ecumenical partnerships (LEPs)

4.117 BAGUPA suggested that 'Christian mission seems to call for both variety and informal local ecumenism. How can the Council for Christian

Unity encourage the Churches together process to avoid inhibiting this but rather promote it?' The Council agrees the need to encourage a varied approach to ecumenical initiatives and seeks to support both formal and informal developments. The Ecumenical Canons of the Church of England (Canons B43 and B44) provide for the sharing of worship appropriate to the different situations. Formal LEPs include shared buildings, shared congregations, local covenants, which hold in partnership a number of local churches, and the sharing of sector ministries and chaplaincies. Alongside this, less formal local arrangements between churches for mission are encouraged.

4.118 In response to a question about the effectiveness or otherwise of LEPs in Urban Priority Areas, the Council suggests that 'shared congregations are nearly always effective once the initial adjustments have been made. Shared congregations are the usual pattern in new housing developments, resulting from ecumenical Church planting, whether in the inner city or in outer estates.'

Relationships with black majority churches

4.119 The Council reports that 'many black majority churches arise from within their own African or Afro-Caribbean culture, which the Church of England has often failed to support. In contrast, in some black majority churches the members are gathered from a very wide area, and engage very little in local mission.' Relationships are developing between the Council and the black majority churches. An observer from the International Ministerial Council of Great Britain sits on the Local Unity Committee and a Church of England representative has been appointed to the IMCGB. It is clear that the Council recognises this as an area for growth in ecumenical relations.

Resources

4.120 In many UPAs resources are scarce; therefore questions about making the best use of these resources have particular pertinence. The Council was asked what role it might play in such discussions. In response, the Council pointed out that 'the local unity secretary with the local unity committee and in regional meetings with diocesan ecumenical officers has frequently considered joint ecumenical deployment. . . particularly where pastoral reorganisation by any church may mean withdrawal from a UPA (for example, deaneries in the Coventry diocese).' It also pointed out the growing number of sector ministries organised ecumenically at diocesan or county level.

4.121   Finally, the Council made it clear that it would welcome closer discussions with BAGUPA on several of these issues and to find out what more it might do to promote good practice in local ecumenical working in UPAs.

BAGUPA comment:

4.122   BAGUPA welcomes this initiative and looks forward to developing these links. It still has questions about the effectiveness of LEPs in urban priority areas, but is aware that this is an issue which needs much closer examination by the Council. In addition, it will be happy to provide the Council with some clear examples of black majority churches of other denominations engaging very effectively with other churches in local mission and action.

> *How much do you know about churches of other denominations in your area? Could you look at some of these questions with members of these churches?*

General Synod Office

4.123   The BAGUPA officer and secretary are members of the staff of this office and remain in close contact with the work of the office as do the Committee for Black Anglican Concerns. The primary function of the office is the servicing of General Synod itself, with attendant oversight of synodical government and the Boards and Councils of Church House. It also services the Policy Committee and the work of the Liturgical and Doctrine commissions.

Participation of people from UPAs in synodical government

4.124   The Office points out that people from UPAs are already actively involved in synodical government, as a glance at the membership of

General Synod and its Standing Committee shows. However, we appreciate that some people (not only from UPAs) may be put off becoming involved, either because of lack of information or because of the particular procedures and styles of synodical government (with their emphasis on public debating and committee skills). We are already attempting to tackle these issues through:

- wider dissemination of information in more popular format about the Synod and other Church matters

- 'tuition' for new members of Synod in how to work the synodical systems

- a more flexible approach to synodical procedures (including revision of the Standing Orders).

4.125 The Office suggested that urban link officers could help by encouraging UPA figures to stand for election.

4.126 BAGUPA asked whether insights from UPA parish development models seeking to include all sections of the population in decision making processes might inform the future development of synodical government. The Office agreed that it would be helpful to have further discussions along these lines.

The workings of General Synod

4.127 A great deal has already been done to simplify the procedures at General Synod itself (including the occasional recasting of standing orders). Moreover, small group work, presentations and wide consultation on key issues are integral to the life of Synod. The Review of Synodical Government Group is considering such issues and BAGUPA is encouraged to make a submission to this body.

4.128 The Office encourages all bodies making written submission to Synod to consider how they can make their reports more accessible (e.g through the use of video and taped material). However, the expense of such an approach is a considerable inhibiting feature of the life of Church House bodies.

The Policy Committee

4.129 The Committee has reviewed from time to time the work of the BAGUPA Officer and will be considering in some detail the results of the

Board review process. In addition, it has agreed the funding of the Officer's post for a further two years, pending reconsideration in the light of the Turnbull Commission report, how best UPA concerns can be reflected in the machinery of the Church at national level.

The Doctrine Commission

4.130 The Commission 'fully supports and should wish to do all that it can to further the Church's work and witness in Urban Priority Areas'. It cites as an example the forthcoming report, *The Mystery of Salvation*, where it has attached considerable importance to the multi-cultural context. 'Other faiths, secularisation, questions of gender, ethnicity and justice have all been prominent features of the background against which our report has been written, and we have treated them in our introductory chapter which is wholly devoted to the context of the modern world'. Specialist advice was sought from Dr Grace Davie with regard to the European Values Survey and to the book *Inner City God* of which she is co-author. These themes are explored later in the report.

4.131 In order to make the report more accessible to those without academic backgrounds, the Commission is exploring the possibility of producing a study guide, similar to that produced for the last Commission report.

The Liturgical Commission

4.132 The Liturgical Commission in 1992 set out its understanding of the function of liturgy in a multi-cultural Church in *A Renewal of Common Prayer* (GS MISC 412). Of particular relevance are chapters 5 (the liturgy in social context), 9 (promoting a common core) and 11 (stability and change; handling liturgy in the parish). The Commission points out that the seriousness with which it takes the issue is evidenced by the fact that it felt it necessary to address these broader questions before embarking on the nitty gritty of liturgical revision.

4.133 *Patterns for Worship* (GS 898), following extensive consultation with UPA congregations, attempted to address issues of staging and presentation of liturgy and adaptation of its forms to suit local contexts. A second edition recently published has a considerably expanded commentary and 'hints and tips' section. One of the elements of the first edition was a *Service of the Word* and this has now received full Synodical authorisation (November 1993); reference to this will show that it

78

consists almost entirely of introduction notes and a balanced 'menu' rather than liturgical text.

4.134   With reference to liturgical language, the Commission points to the importance of story in liturgy and the need for language which is both simple and direct but also allows 'space' for individuals to bring to it deeper levels of meaning.

The Committee for Black Anglican Concerns

4.135   *Faith in the City* and *Living Faith in the City* have documented the circumstances which led to the setting up of the Committee on Black Anglican Concerns (CBAC), as well as its progress in the early years. The annual reports, as well as other Committee publications, provide information about the on-going programme of work.

4.136   The Committee is accountable to the General Synod's Standing Committee. CBAC is mainly responsible for 'considering the programmes, budgets and structures to the Standing Committee, its sub-Committees, the Boards, Councils and other Committees of the General Synod and of the Central Board of Finance, and to provide advice and guidance with a view to supporting efforts for racial justice'. CBAC also works at 'assisting the dioceses in developing strategies for combating racial bias within the Church; encouraging them to make the problems of racism a priority concern in their programmes; and to circulate the best analyses of racism – including theological analyses – and other data helpful for information and education'.

4.137   BAGUPA has asked the Committee to set out some of the main features of its engagements with the central structures of the Church.

CBAC's work within the structures

4.138   The Committee has worked at educating and creating awareness in General Synod and its structures about the nature of institutional racism and how it works.

Strategies

4.139

● The Committee's work is focused, e.g. there are specific terms of reference

- the Committee strives towards achievable results; however because of the nature of the work, these are not always measurable

- CBAC's location within the structures is an advantage, in that it is accountable to General Synod Standing Committee, at the national level of the Church

- the advice and support of the House of Bishops is always sought, especially in relation to large projects. The House is informed regularly of the Committee's progress

- CBAC's collaboration with General Synod Boards and Councils is important. The Committee's terms of reference includes calling Boards and Councils to account in matters that affect black Anglicans.

4.140   Surveys conducted have given confirmatory tools to CBAC. These have been namely:

- the survey on combating racism in the dioceses – publication *Seeds of Hope*

- the survey of black Anglicans' membership of the Church of England in the 1990's which resulted in the report *How we Stand*

- assisting and supporting work in the dioceses.

4.141   The Committee's strength lies mainly in the monitoring role which it performs.

4.142   The under-representation of black people within the synodical structures has been one of the major issues tackled by CBAC. Paragraphs 7.6 and 7.7 of *Living Faith in the City* reported the initiatives which were taken by the House of Bishops, Houses of Clergy and Laity in preparing for the 1990 elections. The elections resulted in an increase from 8 to 14 black members.

4.143   Members of CBAC have had a more direct involvement in the programme of work rather than merely turning up for Committee meetings.

4.144   Although the Committee works at the centre, the emphasis has also been outwardly focused in dioceses, deaneries and parishes.

Work with the CBAC network:
CBAC diocesan link persons

4.145   Bishops were instrumental in enabling the Committee to set up this diocesan network in December 1989, after the failure of the proposed Measure to increase black members of General Synod through co-options.

CBAC Young Black Anglican group

4.146   Bishops helped the Committee to set up this group by nominating representatives from their dioceses.

4.147   This network was developed because there was concern that once structures were more receptive to black participation it would be vital for confident people to come forward. This therefore meant the Committee would endeavour to support and empower black Anglicans to develop their potential and become actively involved at all levels of the Church.

4.148   Within the CBAC network there are 45 diocesan link persons representing 39 dioceses; 22 people represent 20 dioceses in the Young Black Anglican group.

Strategies towards empowerment

4.149   It is important to hear what people are saying as the Committee knows only some of the reasons why many black Anglicans are not participating at all levels of Church life. Our strategies are:

● deliberate targeting and support of younger black Anglicans – under 35 years

● support and training provided to the network, communication links etc.

4.150   The 1994 Black Anglican Celebration for the Decade of Evangelism brought together for the first time ever in the Church of England people in parishes, (black and white) with diocesan bishops, their key advisers, as well as leaders at the centre for a full weekend residential conference. The main objective was to recognise, celebrate and rejoice in the diversity of gifts which black Anglicans bring to the Church of England.

4.151   The pre-celebration pack was effective in helping to develop interest, understanding and discussion on issues of major concern to black Anglicans in Church and society.

4.152   The strength of the network has depended to a large extent on the commitment of the people in the network. In many instances prior to the setting up of CBAC, due to the hurt and alienation which black Anglicans had experienced as a result of racism in the Church, a lethargy of deference prevailed: now a new confidence is emerging.

4.153   This aspect of the work has developed in response to a need, supported by the commitment of Committee members and staff. It has been painstaking developmental work over a period of time. It really is about being interested in people; being willing to share information; to share knowledge of church structures; putting people in touch with people; often acting as a clearing house providing information on publications, training courses, conferences; and developing good practice in combating racism which exists in dioceses, deaneries and parishes.

4.154   It is clear that BAGUPA and CBAC will continue to benefit from close co-operation, although it is important to stress that too close an identification of the two bodies would only reinforce the view that black people are only to be found in inner cities.

BAGUPA comment:

4.155   BAGUPA is grateful to the Synod Office for its response. It is keen to stress that if UPAs are to continue to be prioritised in the life of the Church, then a clear lead from the Policy Committee will be essential (see also the CBF's response). It is grateful to the Committee, too, for the decision to extend the Officer's post for a further two years and looks forward to discussing how such support may be written in to the post-Turnbull structures.

4.156   It was unfortunate that discussions between AGUPA and the Office concerning the encouragement of UPA candidates to stand for Synod, came too late to effect this year's elections; however, BAGUPA will be happy to work with the Office on production of suitable publicity materials for subsequent years. For this year, we have asked link officers to encourage UPA candidates to stand, and to offer support during the election and induction process.

4.157   BAGUPA also looks forward to making a submission to the Synodical Government Review Group and to seeing the outcomes of its report.

> *Do you make sure that candidates from a wide variety of back-grounds stand for election to the PCC or to Diocesan and General Synod? How might meetings of these bodies be made more attractive to those who are not comfortable with formal meetings? Are there other ways of involving people in making decisions?*

Council for the Care of Churches

4.158   Church buildings are a rich resource in many urban priority areas, and the Council for the Care of Churches plays a vital role in ensuring that these can be used to the greatest effect.

Funding issues

4.159   The Council liaises closely with various bodies which may provide financial assistance for parishes considering how best to use their buildings, including the Central Church Fund and the Church Urban Fund, with whom the Council has been involved in the Church Buildings Competition. More recently, the Council has been establishing close links with the Heritage Lottery Fund. It states that 'at present the guidelines for the fund would seem to favour the Grade II listed churches of the nineteenth century, so often found in UPAs, which have not been of sufficiently outstanding quality to make them eligible for English Heritage grants'. While recognising that many churches will not wish to make application to such a fund, such negotiations could provide valuable assistance to many UPA churches.

4.160   In addition, the Council has been pressing for the last four years for further state aid for the maintenance of historic churches. 'Thanks in part to the establishment of a good working partnership between the Church and English Heritage, not only do churches receive more grant aid. . . but English Heritage has become more open to the need on occasion to permit internal adaptation of a church which has been grant-aided in the past. This is particularly relevant in inner city churches.'

Mission and buildings

4.161   The Council points to its report *Mission in Mortar* which has grappled with questions on the role of the church building within the overall mission of the Church. It also points out that within its membership it includes both clergy and architects who have individual experience of inner city problems so that casework is always debated in the context of stewardship of historic churches and the current need of the Church's mission. They say that while 'we recognise the seriousness of problems facing churches in the inner-city, e.g. security, we are anxious to ensure that such areas are not diminished by the loss of their best buildings. There are many examples of inner-city churches which, treated as assets, have come to life in the service of mission.'

Faculty procedures

4.162   In response to questions about the complexity of making faculty applications, the Council states that 'the legal processes which affect the treatment of church buildings were revised in The Care of Churches Measure only a couple of years ago. Tighter legislation has helped to some extent in establishing greater consistency between the attitudes adopted by different Chancellors, though this problem requires further attention. It is still hard for some parishes to follow aspects of the Faculty Jurisdiction but we hope to introduce clarification when the Measure is reviewed. . . If the Faculty Jurisdiction was to be reduced in extent or even abandoned, parishes would still have to fulfil the legal requirements with regard to listed buildings as well as standard planning procedures. They might then find they had jumped out of the frying pan into the fire. Again we would stress that in a time of financial stringency, it is important, even at the risk of a delay, to ensure quality in whatever building work is achieved.'

The Churches Conservation Trust

4.163   The Council states that churches are vested in this trust in the best interests of the nation as a whole and the Church of England. They have to be of exceptional historical and/or architectural interest. It is true that the holdings of the CCT are biased heavily towards the smaller rural church rather than the large urban one. This may change over the next few years. It is possible to return a CCT church to worship and this may indeed provide a solution in some areas of large population.

Design and re-ordering of new buildings

4.164   Although not one of its statutory obligations, the Council does offer advice on the design and re-ordering of new buildings. In particular it stresses the need for both congregations and designers to recognise the appropriateness of particular types of design for particular settings.

4.165   The Council agrees that there are several principles which should be borne in mind when designing or re-ordering an inner city church. These are:

- quality designs and materials
- flexibility
- the need for a holy space
- beauty
- different usable areas
- simple, economic upkeep
- security.

Diocesan Advisory Committees

4.166   DACs have, in many dioceses, taken a close interest in the development and best use of church buildings in UPAs, yet often they are seen as intransigent bodies, as hurdles to be overcome. The Council felt that the role of these bodies should be affirmed and UPA parishes made more aware of the support these committees could offer. It also suggested that much closer links should be forged between the DACs and the Church Urban Fund, to ensure that their expertise was sought and valued in the grant application process.

BAGUPA comment:

4.167   BAGUPA welcomes ongoing dialogue with the Council and wishes to affirm the possible (and in many cases actual) role for DACs in offering support to UPA congregations. While BAGUPA also recognises the essentially complex nature of faculty legislation, it also feels that more could be done to assist congregations which often have few professional people in applying for faculties. It is keen to explore with the Council how this might be achieved; whether through producing simplified guidelines, or through other forms of support from DACs.

Are your church building and hall used as often as they should be? Do people, not just the congregation enjoy going in? What more might be done to use the buildings in the diocese to the full? Is your Diocesan Advisory Council seen as an obstacle or a means of support? Could you find out more about the services they have to offer?

The Communications Committee

4.168   The Communications Committee and its staff have worked very closely with BAGUPA and its officers, particularly in relation to the tenth anniversary of *Faith in the City*.

4.169   *Faith in the City* was effective because it gave people in UPAs a voice. For the first time, people all over the country, inside the churches and out, were aware of the harrowing lives many people were leading not too far away. The task of BAGUPA and of those involved in work with UPAs is, first of all, one of communication. It is therefore very encouraging to have had such a positive response from the Communications Committee to our review.

4.170   In the short term, extensive support is being offered, during this tenth anniversary year, but in the longer term a strategy will be devised and implemented using the Diocesan Communications Officers' network. This will ensure that:

● positive images of life in UPAs are portrayed in publicity initiatives

● people in UPAs receive training in communications skills

● increasingly publicity materials are targeted towards those from a non-book culture (including the use of videos tapes etc)

● the Enquiry Centre will explore the needs of advice centres to assess how it might help them.

BAGUPA comment:

4.171 BAGUPA welcomes the positive and straightforward commitment of the Committee to the needs of UPAs. It looks forward to seeing the finalised strategy and to helping the Committee to implement it.

> *Does your church make sure that all its publications are attractive and understandable to people from a wide range of backgrounds? Do you hear stories and opinions, both painful and inspiring from people and parishes in UPAs?*

Chapter 5

Partners in the city

5.1   *Faith in the City* captured the imagination; it also sparked off a number of initiatives which have developed powerful directions of their own. This chapter describes some organisations which either grew up as a direct result of *Faith in the City*, or whose interests are closely allied with those of urban priority areas. In most cases, BAGUPA has asked the organisations themselves to prepare a piece, with the exception of the Church Urban Fund, who recently reported to General Synod. In this case, BAGUPA felt it was appropriate to follow up that debate with an examination of the relationship between the Fund and the wider recommendations of *Faith in the City*.

Faith in the City
and the Church Urban Fund

5.2   The Church Urban Fund is seen as a powerful advocate by the network of project workers, giving access to partnerships with local authorities and the private sector which would not otherwise be available. Real changes in the lives of some communities has been achieved because CUF has provided much need resources and raised expectations of the projects it supports, requiring that appropriate management structures are in place.

5.3   The Fund has probably received the highest profile of all the initiatives to spring out of *Faith in the City* and BAGUPA believes it is worth examining the relationship between the Fund and the wider *Faith in the City* agenda. After the publication of the report the establishment of the Church Urban Fund captured the imagination of the Church both within urban and non-urban dioceses; some people have argued however, that this had the effect of marginalising the other recommendations of *Faith in the City*.

5.4   The report emphasised the nature of the Church of England as being distinctly middle class:

The growing crisis in our UPAs is reflected in the life of the Church within them. It can be seen in the lack of local leadership, the never-ending struggles with money and buildings, and the powerlessness associated with being divorced from the centres of power. And there is the fact, as we have already stressed, that historically the Church of England has failed to reach or to keep the urban working classes. Submission after submission to us has said that the Church of England's organisation and ministry have been so completely middle class that working class expressions of religion have not been encouraged. *Faith in the City* 4.5, p.74

5.5   This remains the case in many parishes in the Church of England and the report continued:

Unless the whole Church can be persuaded to take seriously the challenge and the plight of the Church in the UPAs, it will cease to be the Church of the whole people. Yet well-intentioned appeals to the wider Church will not necessarily achieve a greater commitment of the whole Church to the UPAs. The obstacles to effective change are deeply entrenched. *Faith in the City* 5.77, p.100ff

5.6   The report cited as reasons for this entrenchment, the lack of personal experience of UPAs; a 'don't want to know attitude', an inability to relate to UPAs, a feeling of helplessness, and a 'we've enough problems of our own' attitude. Yet the report felt that the Church of England should respond to the challenge:

. . . we must firmly recognise that the Church is, and has the potential to be even more, a major force for good in our society. The Church as a whole can promote a more sensitive climate of public opinion. . . all Christians should take part in promoting that common good which would benefit the UPAs and their Churches, by public commitment to social welfare and justice, to good education, housing, and health for all. It is important for Christians to show themselves committed as 'members one of another' as citizens, as well as within the structures of the Church. *Faith in the City* 5.85-86, p.102

5.7   It is against this understanding of the Church of England as it was in 1985, and its potential recognised by the report, that the recommendation for a Church Urban Fund should be seen.

5.8   The Fund was set up to provide an 'explicit priority' for UPAs in order that the Church might challenge the state to respond to the needs of the poor:

> In the secular world, the Government has retained an Urban Programme, running at over £300 million per annum, despite imposing cuts in the revenue and capital expenditure by UPA local authorities. As we note later in our report, we believe this sum to be inadequate given the scale of the problem. But it is difficult for the Church of England to criticise the inadequacy of this expenditure, when the Church itself at national level has done little to give explicit priority to the UPAs. *Faith in the City* 7.87, p.162

5.9   The implication of this statement is that the establishment of an 'explicit priority' in terms of the resources available to UPA parishes – the Church Urban Fund – confers a far more credible voice against the inadequacies of Government policy. It will also provide the basis on which 'the Church as a whole can promote a more sensitive climate . . .' (*Faith in the City* 5.85) and the evidence of what constitutes 'that common good which would benefit the UPAs and their Churches' (*Faith in the City* 5.86) This lies at the very heart of the relationship between the urban link officer network and the Church Urban Fund. Yet it is in this area that the Church of England, the urban link officer network and the Church Urban Fund have singularly failed to make an impression on the changing landscape of values and political ideologies applied to UPAs. From 'City Challenge', through the erosion of funding for the Urban Programme and the introduction of the Single Regeneration Budget, the Government has changed the way in which it has sought to respond to the problem of urban deprivation and has demanded, successfully, that other agencies adopt their values almost without challenge.

5.10   The recommendation for a Church Urban Fund (*Faith in the City* 7.88-94) recognised the need to involve dioceses in the care of their own UPAs, so that a great deal of the recommendation was addressed to the dioceses themselves:

(i)   prepare a *diocesan UPA strategy*, based on;

(ii) analysis of *Census and other data* to determine the number and location of UPA parishes together with the results of local Church audit undertaken in selected areas at parish or deanery level; to

(iii) determine the *priorities for ministry* and mission in the UPA parishes and areas, in terms of staff and buildings;

(iv) consider how far these priorities might be met by *redirection of existing resources* (taking into account the likelihood of, and potential for, increased levels of giving);

(v) propose a list of projects or schemes which rate as priorities, but which could go ahead only with extra financial assistance. These could either be *capital* (e.g. adaption of an inappropriate UPA church *building*) *or current* (e.g. a detached youth worker or secretarial support for a team ministry). *Faith in the City* (c) p.163

5.11   It was also envisaged that the Fund itself would accumulate a wealth of information which could be used by the wider Church:

> *Monitoring and Review.* Some central monitoring of schemes on a regular basis would be desirable, both to ensure that Fund monies were spent on the basis greed, and to *facilitate exchange of information and good practice. Faith in the City* (f) p.164

5.12   Such aspirations have not yet been achieved. It is only in recent years that some dioceses have taken seriously the need to develop strategies towards their own UPAs The Sheffield Hallam report *Hope in the City?* has recognised this and the need to use the wealth of information at its disposal for a wider reflection by the whole Church; the *Hope in the City* Working Party set up by the Fund in response to the report picks up several of these themes.

Implications for the Church Urban Fund

5.13   *Hope in the City* drew out a number of implications for the Fund:

- CUF at the centre can encourage dioceses to adopt a strategic and supportive role in relation to the Fund's local initiatives. *Hope in the City?* p.6

- priorities may need to be decided in the context of a more theological reflection on the role of CUF, in the light of both the challenges posed by *Faith in the City* and also the immediate and unfolding experience of local CUF projects and their surrounding communities. *Hope in the City?* p.7

- we are aware that the Fund has an enormously valuable and unique resource of information on individual projects which combines material obtained through its regular monitoring of projects as well as independent evaluations . . . Such information should be made available to dioceses and be an important resource for the wider Church. *Hope in the City?* Working Party Report 3.36, p.1

- In our view the Fund should be doing much more to fertilise the theology and mission of the Church and the understanding of the Church and wider society about the realities of life in UPAs. It's a major educative and prophetic role, which we would see built into the operation of the Fund that has not happened before . . . *Hope in the City?* Working Party 3.39, p.16

5.14   That it 'has not happened before' is a measure of the continuing difficulty of the Church of England in coming to terms with the realities of life in UPAs. *Faith in City* recognised that 'well-intentioned appeals to the wider Church will not necessarily achieve a greater commitment of the whole Church to the UPAs'. Given the background of the Church of England and the attitudes already mentioned it is not surprising that the wider agenda of *Faith in the City* has been difficult to communicate.

5.15   The opportunity to make some tangible contribution to the difficulties of UPAs was always likely to be more attractive than having to think through the difficult issues of powerlessness and poverty. A monetary contribution is far easier than a change in our views and attitudes towards society. This has been the experience of a number of charitable institutions.

Implications for the Church of England

5.16   *Hope in the City?* also devoted attention to some implications for the Church of England:

- much has been achieved in the first six years of CUF's operation. However, the problems faced by people in many inner cities and outer estates remain acute, and in many cases are actually worse than when *Faith in the City* was published.

- a wide gulf remains between the realities of life in the UPAs and the experiences of the wider Church. What continuing priority can be accorded to CUF and more general 'Faith in the City issues' in the light of present pressures upon the Church and the demands upon its apparently diminishing material resources?

- CUF is largely consistent with an earlier 'Anglican social tradition', but much of its activity sets aside issues of powerlessness and political marginalisation raised, but not developed, in *Faith in the City*. UPAs with high statistical measures of deprivation will still have high levels of deprivation even with the presence of several CUF projects. If the Fund's resources are to be used to greatest effect, issues of power and politics cannot be ignored. *Hope in the City?* p.7

- we believe the initiatives supported by the Fund provide both information, the rationale and the authority for Church bodies to speak out on such issues. *Hope in the City* Working Party 3.40, p.16

5.17   As has been noted earlier, in recent years dioceses, especially those with a large number of UPAs, have begun to develop strategies which give priority to deprived urban areas. Yet there is still a lack of information which will allow the whole Church to reflect on the issues of poverty and powerlessness, and very few non-urban Dioceses have any strategic plans towards urban dioceses.

In conclusion

5.18   If the Church of England is to continue to respond to the challenge of *Faith in the City*, the need for CUF to disseminate its wealth of information is crucial. BAGUPA looks forward to working with the Fund as it seeks to develop this new role. The success of the Church in raising funds cannot be an excuse for not confronting the causes which contribute to the continuing presence of disadvantage in our society. How can the Church challenge the nation when it avoids the issues itself?

Inner Cities Religious Council

5.19   The proposal for an Inner Cities Religious Council was announced at a meeting organised by the Urban Bishops' Group at General Synod in November 1991 by Mr Robert Key MP, then Parliamentary Under-Secretary of State at the Department of the Environment.

5.20   Against the background of 'disturbances' on depressed housing estates during that autumn, he had written to the Archbishop of Canterbury urging that the Church and Government should find a better way of working together for the good of local communities in inner cities and outer housing estates. His proposal of collaboration led to the setting up of an Inner Cities Religious Council, chaired by a Government Minister, with members drawn from across the main faith communities living in inner city and deprived urban areas in England, was welcomed by the Archbishop and as a sign of the Church of England's commitment, he agreed to second the Revd Chris Beales to act as its Secretary.

5.21   The original aims of the ICRC were to act as a focal point for faith communities to meet with Government and discuss policy issues of concern to them, to share information about Government programmes and to promote the development of practical local initiatives.

5.22   The ICRC has met three times a year for over three years. Participants come from the Christian (including black-led churches), Hindu, Jewish, Muslim and Sikh communities. It now has a number of women members. Attendance is good, conflict is real and well handled, collaboration is increasing all the time.

5.23   The Council has now organised eight regional conferences which provide a forum for dialogue between faith communities and with the main voluntary and government sponsored agents of urban regeneration. Each conference is chaired by a Council member, usually addressed by the Chairman of the ICRC, who is Parliamentary Secretary of State for the Environment. The programme allows times for group work on a district council/borough basis and highlights good practice.

5.24   There is a programme of follow-up work where Regional Conferences have been held. The content of this is responsive to the wishes of local faith community groups. The work comes under four main headings:

- enabling faith community leaders to meet and contact each other. This has included setting up local 'Councils of Faiths'
- assisting Government organisations to work with faith communities
- assisting practical joint faith initiatives
- assisting single faith initiatives.

5.25   The Secretariat serves as an advice resource on faith dimensions of urban regeneration to government. This is a two-way process between those in Government departments asking the Secretariat for advice and the Secretariat advising those responsible for policy areas. An example of this is the advice put out to City Challenges on collaboration with faith communities.

5.26   The Secretariat also serves as a source of information and advice to faith communities seeking to develop their programmes. For example, CUF have received financial assistance for their research programme.

5.27   The Secretariat works closely with the Archbishop's staff, the Board of Mission, Board of Social Responsibility, BAGUPA, CUF advisers on inter-faith issues, Churches' Commission on Racial Justice, the Inter-Faith Network, Linking Up and the Ecumenical Urban Forum and others.

5.28   Financially the Church of England contributes one-third of the Secretary's salary, with contributions from the black-led churches, Roman Catholic and Methodist Churches. The Government meets all support costs (two other colleagues, the contractors that run the conferences and undertake the follow-up work). This is currently in the region of £200,000 per annum.

A continuing challenge

5.29   If we are to avoid serious conflict in the streets of our cities, we need to work towards active collaboration for the welfare of all by all. Justice must not only be something that all can receive, but which all are able to strive for. Thee must be no doubt that one can be British and fully so, as Muslim, Sikh, Hindu, Jewish, as well as Christian. There are still many barriers to participatory citizenship, and some of the needs that the ethnic minority faith communities struggle with are heartbreaking. Some of the responses are inspirational.

The Revd David Horn (Secretary to the Council)

The Archbishop's Urban Theology Group

Origins of the Group

5.30   When *Living Faith in the City* reviewed the progress of *Faith in the City*, and was debated in General Synod in 1990, there was a chapter on the theological foundations of the original report. This chapter raised five questions about the understanding of theology. These were as follows:

● the role and task of theology, including the place of black, urban, feminist and other inductive theology

● the use of biblical material

● the debate about the report concerned the nature of the Kingdom of God, justice, dialogue with other faiths, etc.

● the nature of theological training, especially (but not only) of ordinands in theological colleges

● the theological significance of Church Urban Fund projects established since the original report.

5.31   *Living Faith in the City* argued for the need to hold academic theology in constructive tension with emerging local theologies. An example of the latter is given in a quotation from Laurie Green's book *Power to the Powerless. Living Faith in the City* also pointed to Christian hesitancy about the city (paragraph 2:6), which it felt needed to be overcome. It hoped for a new vision of the City of God, of liberation, and of witness which was biblically based and aware of the social reality of our society. Therefore its recommendations were that 'a small group of theologians (maximum five) should be commissioned by the Archbishops to produce, within a given period (perhaps between five and seven years) two volumes [i] a textbook on urban theology. . . and [ii] a reader in urban theology.' (paragraph 2:21).

The Group is established

5.32   Prebendary Pat Dearnley approached Revd Dr Peter Sedgwick to convene such a group in 1990. The Group first met in January 1991 and was composed of Professor D. Ford (Cambridge), Bishop L. Green (then parish priest of Poplar, later Bishop of Bradwell), Revd C. Hendrickse (Liverpool), Mrs R. McCurry (a member of the *Faith in the City*

Commission and Trustee of the Church Urban Fund), Dr Al Mcfadyen (Leeds), Revd Dr M. Northcott (Edinburgh), Revd N. Thompson (North London), and Sister M. Walsh (Wolverhampton). Peter Sedgwick convened the Group while Revd Alan Davis (who succeeded Preb. Dearnley) assisted them and Bishop Tom Butler provided a link with the House of Bishops. Mrs Gill Moody later replaced Alan Davis, and Revd Sue Hope (Sheffield) took the place of Clarry Hendrickse.

5.33   The Group has met three times a year since January 1991 and was launched by the Archbishop of Canterbury in January 1993. Integral to its existence was the completion of a textbook on urban theology and the preparation of an accompanying reader.

The Textbook: *God in the City*

5.34   Our first book reflects the way in which we have worked as a group. We decided right at the start that a group of five people was too small. Instead we took four university theologians, three parish clergy and two lay people and set up a debate between us on the nature of theology, on how the Church has evolved local theologies and on how the social context has deteriorated in recent years. The process of building a close trust was, and is, very important for us: we shared much pain and achieved an unusual degree of understanding of very different positions, theologically and socially. There is much here that the Church can learn from. A second section is earthed in Poplar and Wolverhampton, telling as well the story of two people's lives in conversation form. Only then do we attempt constructive theology. Each chapter was agreed on by the groups as a topic which was worth writing about. Next the topic was brainstormed as a group. Only then did the author write a first draft, which was considered by the Group at its next meeting. After lengthy discussion, a revised text was circulated to about fifty respondents in urban areas. Finally, at our last meeting, yet another revision took account of these comments. We have also been addressed as a group by well-known urban theologians, including Revd Ken Leech, Mrs Elaine Appelbee and Bishop Peter Selby.

5.35   So what did we write about? We wrote on sin and praise, and transformation. We included children, the black experience and sanctuary as important. We looked at sexuality, estrangement and enterprise, and violence, as well as a sense of place. Finally, we wondered whether the Church could overcome its fear of the city. It is a cultural description of life in the modern city today, which sees the task of the Church as being a witnessing, caring and prophetic body which worships Jesus Christ in the midst of great poverty and enormous vibrancy of human life. So the book celebrates the city as part of God's creation.

What we have not done

5.36　Although Bishop Green is a former Principal of the Aston Training Scheme, and Professor Ford is Regius Professor of Divinity at Cambridge, we have not addressed the question of theological training directly. Instead we have concentrated on writing a constructive theology. The reader will certainly be read in theological colleges, but the task of reflecting on theological training is, we believe, best helped by showing how theology can be done well by a collaborative group. So it is our way of working (process) which is as important as our product, and we hope that it will be significant for the wider Church, and not just the urban one, as it seeks to proclaim the love of God in the City.

Revd Dr Peter Sedgwick, Convenor of the Group

The Churches National Housing Coalition

5.37　The Coalition was established in December 1991 as a result of a series of consultations convened by Church Action on Poverty and the National Churches Housing Consultation 1990. To date, over 500 organisations have joined the Coalition, including all the major denominations 'headquartered' in England, the Church in Wales, the Church of Scotland and the Free Church Federal Council.

How we see the housing problem

5.38　Because housing is a fundamental human right as well as a basic human need, and the resources required to provide decent housing for everyone are limited, we require of any Government a housing policy which is economically and socially responsible. But what we have inherited is a system whose structural flaws actually tend both to promote the inefficient use of scarce resources and to entrench inequalities in society. At the very time when house prices are falling and the market is glutted with unsold properties, rents are rising far in excess of the rate of inflation, and homelessness is continuing to rise.

5.39   We are very aware of the range of initiatives taken by the Government to alleviate the problem of homelessness, particularly in central London. However welcome as such initiatives are, they fail to address the structural flaws in our housing system. Where the Churches National Housing Coalition believes that major housing policy changes are needed is in the area of the supply of accommodation for rent at affordable prices.

5.40   The Churches have a significant contribution to make to addressing these issues through both practical response and political engagement. The Coalition mission is to strengthen and develop the Churches in their prophetic witness and engagement in the field of housing and homelessness, in order to achieve housing policies based on a vision of an inclusive society in which decent, appropriate and affordable housing is available to all.

CNHC's achievements to date

5.41

- organising a national lobby of Parliament in December 1992 in which over 3000 people from churches across the country participated. A petition, signed by almost million people, was also delivered to Parliament by the Coalition in March 1993.

- encouraging Churches to reflect on the relationship between Christian faith, worship and action on homelessness, through an annual Homelessness Sunday. In 1994 over 14,000 copies of the special order of service were distributed for use by local churches.

- promoting the establishment of over 30 rent/guarantee schemes to rehouse homeless people in the private rented sector, through the publication of a handbook, and a series of training events across the country.

- publishing the *Churches and Housing Handbook,* launched by the Archbishop of Canterbury in November 1994, and organising over a dozen regional seminars for key church decision-makers, to promote the use of church land and property for affordable housing.

- co-ordinating the Churches' response to the Government's Homelessness Review during 1994, which with others lead to two of the most damaging aspects of the proposals being withdrawn. However, the government remains committed to the main principles contained in the review: a Housing White Paper was published in June 1995 and legislation is expected before the end of the year.

The Current situation

5.42   The current housing context is one of changing and growing housing need, continued public ignorance of the true extent of the scale of the problem, declining housing investment, and a proposed legislative programme which is likely to considerably exacerbate existing pressure on both homeless families and young people. Evidence from agencies working with young homeless people reveals that whilst the recession has slowed the drift of young people to London and the South East, it is forcing up youth homelessness – especially amongst vulnerable groups – across the country. At the same time there is some evidence of compassion fatigue: that homelessness, even amongst young people, is increasingly becoming an 'accepted' (if not acceptable) social fact.

5.43   CNHC's main theme for the next year is 'People Need Homes': a national programme of local research and action on homelessness by church groups. It is based on the premise that the most effective means of addressing these problems is by bringing the issues down to a local level, revealing the impact of homelessness and the policies that restrict access to housing on young people and families in peoples' own towns and communities.

Niall Cooper, Director CNHC

Church Action on Poverty

5.44   Church Action on Poverty was formed in 1982 as an ecumenical response to increasing levels of poverty in the UK. Our main aims have been to:

- develop a theology which relates to contemporary society and in particular to the increasing levels of social and economic exclusion

100

- raise awareness about the causes, extent and impact of poverty on individuals and communities

- campaign for changes in public attitudes and policies in order to ensure lasting solutions to the problems of the poorest people in society.

5.45   CAP has always worked to build up a strong and active grass roots membership, especially in those areas where poverty levels are highest.

5.46   Key achievements and developments are:

- the Consultation for, and publication of, the CAP Declaration *Hearing the Cry of the Poor* (1989) – over 100,000 copies were circulated

- the initial co-ordination of the Churches National Housing Coalition (1991)

- the organisation of six national poverty consultations involving representatives of a wide range of church-based organisations and agencies (1988 onwards)

- the three year 'Local People National Voice' initiative which has given people in poverty an opportunity to speak out at local and national level (1993 onwards)

- opening the CAP Parliamentary office (1994)

- taking over the co-ordination of Unemployment Sunday from Church Action With the Unemployed (1995)

- a wide variety of other activities including: regular national conferences and training events, meetings with Government ministers, evidence given to Parliamentary Select Committees and the Social Security Advisory Committee, regular press briefings on poverty trends and their impact on society.

5.47   CAP is widely regarded as a reliable source of information and analysis. However, we have not achieved our greater goal of changing values and attitudes either in society at large or the Church. The number living in poverty has more than doubled since 1982. We want to see all policies measured against their impact on the most vulnerable groups, but there is no sign yet of the political will to do so. Similarly, although poverty is an important concern for many Christians, it is still not seen as a social justice issue central to the Church.

5.48   A more encouraging trend is the increasing importance attached to the need to listen to those who experience poverty directly. The 'Local People National Voice' campaign has been greeted with enthusiasm both by those who have at last had a chance to speak out and those more comfortably off who have heard their voices and felt the need to act. A significant future event for CAP, therefore, is the National Poverty Hearing on 19 March 1996 when we hope a wide cross-section of decision-makers from the Churches, Government, business and voluntary sectors will come to listen.

5.49   For the future, in addition to providing the usual services to our members and supporters – provided we can raise the necessary funds – we aim to:

- consolidate and develop both the 'Local People National Voice' and Parliamentary work, in particular to increase our capacity to support and train local people to use media opportunities

- increase our networking in Europe

- work more closely with Third World development agencies on the links between poverty in so-called developed and developing nations

- develop more resources for churches, including worship materials.

Paul Goggins, National Co-ordinator, CAP

Churches Commission for Racial Justice

5.50   The Churches Commission for Racial Justice (CCRJ) officially came into existence on 1 September 1992. It has 16 Member Church bodies, represented by 20 Commissioners, and others have members nominated by the CCBI, including Christian Aid, the Irish Council of Churches and the Scottish Churches' Agency for Racial Justice. The Commission has built on the twenty years of work of the former British Council of Churches' Community and Race Relations Unit (1971 to 1992).

5.51   The Commission was formed 'to monitor trends in race relations in British society, to encourage the exchange of information among the churches regarding these trends and to co-ordinate response'. The Commission also administers the Ecumenical Fund for Racial Justice, focussed on overcoming racial discrimination by supporting local, national and European organisations in these fields.

5.52   The main areas of work the Commission has addressed are immigration and access, the criminal justice system and especially racial violence, and race equality in employment. The first of these has taken the most time and resources. The CCRJ co-ordinated the Churches' response to the Asylum and Immigration Appeals Act when it was making its way through Parliament in 1992/3 and has been monitoring its effects since, especially the increasing number of asylum-seekers detained in prisons and detention centres.

5.53   The other major immigration issue has become deportations, especially of families who have lived here for ten or even fifteen years. Many cases have been brought by the black majority churches, including some of their pastors and their families. In response to this, and to the death of Joy Gardner while police were attempting to deport her in July 1993, the CCRJ evolved the principle of amnesty whereby families who had lived here for more than five years, with a child born here of at least two, should be allowed to stay. This was supported by the Church Representatives Meeting of the CCBI, and a petition throughout the churches during most of 1994 received 30,000 signatures. The Home Office continues to refuse to discuss the idea. Partly because of this and because of what has been happening in local churches, the Commission has developed a position on sanctuary which it is currently circulating among the churches for their response.

5.54   With respect to racial violence, the CCRJ was active with other organisations in 1993/4 in seeking to get the law strengthened. During 1993/4 the Commission developed an education pack for churches on racial harassment, *One Race*, and this was launched by the Archbishop of Canterbury, Cardinal Hume, the Methodist President and others in May 1994. A pack for schools is now in preparation.

5.55   The Commission put to the CCBI in early 1994 the idea of a Racial Justice Sunday, to be celebrated on the second Sunday of September in all churches. This was accepted and the first Racial Justice Sunday took place on 10 September 1995. The CCRJ has also attempted to keep abreast of developments at European Union level and is an active member of the Churches Commission for Migrants in Europe, based in Brussels. It is supporting the campaign on 'The Starting Point', which is a proposed amendment to the Treaty of Maastricht which will outlaw racial discrimination in the EU. In addition, the CCRJ has developed contacts with the Inner Cities Religious Council and secular bodies in the field, including the Commission for Racial Equality, and the Asylum Rights Campaign and the Standing Conference on Race Equality for Europe (SCORE).

Revd David Haslam, Associate Secretary for Racial Justice

The Ecumenical Urban Forum

5.56   There are two aspects of working within the churches in cities which are often undervalued. One is to do with the long haul of building networks and putting people in touch with each other. The other is to do with sustaining opportunities for Church staff to meet.

5.57   The reason why such groups are important is that we need continuity and security. We need to learn about each other. We owe it to those who have gone before us to learn from their stories. We owe it to those at local Church level to get the best shared experience and most creative insights that we can.

5.58   So some of us have to channel our passion and drive about urban issues, mission, theology, politics into the routine tasks of mailings, networking, regular contact points. Some of the energy has to go into administration, structures, staff consultation – seeking to win resources.

5.59   The Ecumenical Urban Forum, which began in about 1985, is such a group. It meets twice a year. We are national and Church agency staff who are engaged in urban mission. Most of us are answerable to committees which include people in local churches and most of us visit and work with local urban churches. We come at urban mission along many routes: Church growth and new churches, urban issues including racial justice and poverty, urban spirituality, the survival and development of local established churches, funding and linking with the Department of the Environment's Inner Cities Religious Council, and new styles of mission and ministry.

5.60   The Forum includes people from the Church of England, Roman Catholic, Methodist, Baptist and United Reformed Churches, Scripture Union and Frontier Youth Trust, All Asia Christian Consultative Group, Church Action on Poverty, Churches Community Work Alliance,

Committee for Racial Justice and the Council of Churches for Britain and Ireland.

5.61 We have agreed, and have stayed with, three aims:

- we understand urban mission to mean outreach by the Church (through evangelism, social caring, political justice and concern for the environment) in our cities. This understanding contains within it a commitment to the poor and disadvantaged and to the hope that cities can be good places in which to live and places in which God is to be found.

- we are committed to promoting urban mission within the whole Church, ecumenically and in terms of the Church's response to society and Government. This involves a concern for policy, priorities and resources for urban mission.

- we intend to meet twice each year as staff working 'at national level' for the purpose of sharing information, planning appropriate action and events, relating to Church and other structures. This will be done with the minimum of formal structure.

We meet, share information, do business and make dates, plan to work together or not to duplicate work. Often it is all fairly routine, but sometimes conversations flare with excitement and insights. At best we support and inspire one another.

The Revd Tony Holden (Convenor of the Group)

Churches' Community Work Alliance

5.62 The Alliance was formed as the successor to the British Council of Churches Community Resource Unit after a process of widespread consultation. It formally commenced work on 1 February 1991. The major external funder for the first three years was the Jerusalem Trust, with additional funding coming from the initiating group of Churches – the Church of England, the Roman Catholic Church in England and Wales, the United Reformed Church and the Presbyterian Church in Wales. Further contributions were also made from other denominations. The Alliance received charitable status in 1992.

5.63 The Alliance believes that Church community work should be built on a vision of the Church as an agent of social change. It sees community work as a vehicle for affirming the Kingdom of God in human affairs. Church community work is of the Kingdom because it is committed to social justice and is not afraid of costly involvement with people. Because Church-related community work is committed to justice and to change, it is a challenge both to an insular Church and an uncaring society.

5.64   The aims of the Churches' Community Work Alliance are:

• to support and encourage individual and collective vocations and initiatives for community work in the life and mission of the Churches

• to contribute theological insights relevant to the Churches' mission and involvement in community work of all kinds, and their response to social and economic change

• to foster and develop good community work practice

• to provide guidance for community work projects

5.65   The Alliance is active in each of the four countries of the United Kingdom and in the Republic of Ireland. It works across denominational boundaries and with both Church based and non-Church based institutions. It is a partnership between the Churches, networks of Church community workers and Christian organisations committed to community development. The Alliance holds biennial conferences which bring together Christians engaged in community ministry. It produces newsletters and briefing papers on themes relevant to the theology, theory and practice of Church community work. Groups within the Alliance work on specific community related issues, and the organisation contributes both to denominational thinking and to the work of the Council of Churches for Britain and Ireland.

Brian Ruddock, Co-ordinating Secretary

Urban Theology Unit

5.66   The Urban Theology Unit in Sheffield was founded in 1969. It is an independent ecumenical educational charity, responsible to its 350 members, and serviced by a small core staff of mainly part-time urban ministers and workers. Additionally, some 30 ministers and others work as spare time lecturers. UTU co-operates with Anglican UPA officers and dioceses with courses and resources, as it does with other corresponding agencies.

5.67   Since 1972 it has organised a yearly 'Study Year' for community work experience and biblical/theological/missional study and reflection, designed to help in the formation of vocations to urban work and ministry. Since 1972 it has also conducted an 'Urban Ministry Course' in many parts of the country, which has serviced hundreds of urban and other ministers. Both continue with new groups commencing each September.

5.68   To service these, John Vincent's *Situation Analysis* was compiled in 1978. This formed the core of the 'Parish Audit' in *Faith in the City*. Urban Theology has been developed through *Stirrings* (Epworth 1976); *Gospel from the Poor* (UTU 1984); *Good News in Britain* (UTU 1994); and in Vincent's books, *Starting All Over Again* (WCC 1981), *Into the City* (Epworth 1982), *Radical Jesus* (Marshall Pickering 1986), *Britain in the 90s* (Methodist Publishing House 1989) and *British Liberation Theology*. UTU also publishes many booklets on urban issues.

5.69   UTU was much involved in the Methodist campaign for 'Mission Alongside the Poor' inaugurated by the Methodist Conference and in *Two Nations, One Gospel* (Methodist Church/UTU 1981). At present UTU is one of the four organisations co-operating in a Working Group on the Cities, the report of which is to be published, after wide ecumenical consultation, in June 1996.

5.70   In the future, UTU envisages:

• developing further its ecumenical involvements. Half its members are Anglican, with growing Roman Catholic participation continuing co-operation in national and regional urban concerns and campaigns, and assisting the development of ecumenical urban action-study centres pursuing the growth of urban theology, and publication of it, especially harvesting the fruits of people's bible studies and popular urban Christianity

• continuing courses and academic expertise to support these. Current part-time courses are: diploma in Community Ministry, diploma in Theology and Mission, diploma in Ministry (basic ordained ministry training), plus courses for degrees awarded by Sheffield University, notably BMin (basic ministerial logical training), MMin (in-service ministry), MPhil and PhD (in contextual, urban and liberation theologies).

John Vincent, Director

BAGUPA comment:

5.71 These bodies, some of which developed in direct response to *Faith in the City* provide a means of support for urban priority areas. There are many other similar organisations, some national, others with a more local brief. However, many of these bodies have one major problem which threatens the valuable work they do: they have very little money and an insecure future, looking to where the next grant is coming from. It is important that the Church recognises their work, and that parishes, dioceses and the central Church structures are aware of what they achieve and are committed to ensuring their long-term existence. Long-term financial support for such agencies is a critical question for the Church, in terms of its support for UPAs.

5.72 In particular BAGUPA acknowledges the need to continue to support, sustain and develop Church related community work which will include a reassessment of the allocation of resources at parish, diocesan and national levels.

Chapter 6

Staying in the city

6.1   Commenting on the ABM response above (paragraphs 4.56-7), we said:

> Are people living and working in urban priority areas just one among many interest groups, pressing for time, in competition with other equally vocal bodies? In some respects this may be true, but this highlights that basic question: in what sense are people living in places of extreme deprivation accorded a priority within the life of the Church?
>
> Most clergy who have experienced UPA ministry describe its powerful formative influence on their development. Direct engagement with the poor sharpens up a Gospel often clouded in other areas by self-interest and comfort. The unshrouded Gospel of Christ's passion and resurrection is daily lived out in the experiences of people living in extreme poverty. This is at the heart of the priority which the Church should be according to urban priority areas: a priority which recognises the value of UPAs to the whole Church itself and which directs resources to that end.
>
> UPAs as interest groups? or a living expression of Christ's presence with humankind?

6.2   People in urban parishes of extreme deprivation must continue to have priority in the life of the Church and nation: a priority because they have overwhelming needs and because they have been denied access to positions of power which might allow them to make a real difference, but also because where the Church touches the materially poor, sick and outcasts, then it is at its sharpest. The rest of the Church should hear this Gospel and respond to it, and meet its own poverty wherever this exists.

6.3   *Faith in the City* taught the Church that wherever it operates it must be outward looking; it must recognise and meet Christ in its own poverty and those of the people it serves. The Church can no longer stand apart from society, it must see God in the culture of those of other faiths and none, it must receive as much as it gives.

6.4   *Faith in the City* is teaching the Church that its primary aim must be to help people, through the life of local churches to relate their faith to their daily lives in thought, prayer, decision-making and action.

In conclusion

6.5   If the Church of England is committed to *staying in the city*, then it must ensure that it does indeed give priority to deprived urban areas.

6.6   BAGUPA therefore recommends that:

1   The Church, through its central, diocesan and local structures, drawing on expertise, theology and prayer, should:

    a   continue to give priority to UPAs both in its own life and seek it in the life of the nation

    b   celebrate the gifts and achievements of urban communities and learn from them

    c   seek to understand the context in which churches in UPAs operate. In particular it should:

        ●   seek means of providing adequate information including Census and other data to help the Church understand the society it serves

        ●   continue to ensure that doctrine and liturgy reflect the creative diversity of cultures given by God.

2   In particular General Synod should:

    a   request the Policy Committee and the Budget Committee to give explicit priority to UPAs in its budgeting procedures

    b   request the House of Bishops, the Church Commissioners and the Central Board of Finance to seek a structural mechanism for ensuring the financial interdependence of the Church, so that UPAs do not become dependent either on a bidding process or individual acts of generosity

    c   through appropriate Boards, Councils and networks enter into dialogue with Government on the disturbing findings of independent research in the several areas of social and economic policy described in chapter 1; campaign for the adoption of more effective policies, more just allocation of resources and full participation by the local communities concerned in order to bring about sustainable change.

> *What have you learned since* Faith in the City? *What do you want to say about this to the Church and your diocese, deanery and parish?*

Appendix 1

The following statements have been adopted by the Bishops' Advisory Group on Urban Priority Areas, following consultation with urban link officers. They are based on similar statements adopted in September 1995, by Christian Aid in respect of their work in Britain and overseas.

Statement of faith

Responding to God's presence and action in creation, we believe that:

† God's project for creation is that all should contribute to and participate in the feast of life

† the life, death and resurrection of Jesus Christ are, for us, essential signs pointing to this abundant life

† one of these signs is that God puts poor and oppressed people first and we should too

† struggle and justice are central to God's activity

† in order to enter into abundant life, we are called to engage together in this struggle

† God gives gifts to all people, individually and in groups; unless all are open to receive the gifts and insights God has entrusted to those in UPAs all are deprived and the body of Christ cannot be whole.

Statement of intent

Recognising that in many ways, conditions for people in UPAs have worsened since 1985, we will:

† work for the welfare of the cities, believing that in their welfare we find our true common wealth as a nation

† strengthen our support for the poorest communities as they struggle for justice

† campaign for a transfer of resources, including money and staff, towards UPAs

† encourage and resource those who care deeply about urban deprivation, so that they need not feel helpless to change it

† challenge those who do not care

† while churches are a starting point, seek common ground and ways to co-operate with people of all faiths or none, who side with the poor and the oppressed

† remain critical of prevailing social and economic systems, especially free-market capitalism, and challenge Government and national institutions to listen to the poor in UPAs and take appropriate action

† respond to anger, social dis-ease, unrest and crime

† work to ensure that people from UPAs are included in the prevailing systems, so that they can gain from them, resist and reform them

† help urban communities to protect their cultures

† celebrate and learn from the gifts and achievements of urban communities.

Appendix 2

Link officers and diocesan strategies

Early in 1993, dioceses were sent guidelines on the production of a diocesan strategy.

In June 1995 link officers sent a questionnaire to dioceses, which sought to elicit information concerning the progress of dioceses in producing such strategies. In addition link officers were asked questions about finance and about their own role in the diocese. The results are shown below. We have not made distinctions here between dioceses with many UPAs and those with few, believing that the questions posed were relevant to all.

Strategies

Of the 27 dioceses which have replied to date:

7 say that they have specific UPA strategies (2 of which are presently being up-dated)

3 have a significant UPA component as part of a wider diocesan strategy

4 are in the process of preparing a specific strategy

3 are in the process of ensuring a significant UPA component as part of a wider diocesan strategy

10 dioceses say that they do not have such a strategy.

The majority of those who claim that no strategy exists, are dioceses with very few urban areas. However, it is clear that in many of these dioceses there exists an understanding, in some cases agreed, in others unwritten, that it is part of the task of less urban dioceses to support ministry in places of urban deprivation.

'Although no official policy exists', writes one link officer in a diocese with no official UPAs, 'the Bishop has taken some bold moves in creating new parishes and locating clergy in urban deprivation areas – at a time when the diocese is in financial difficulties. Some of these have been designated 'mission' parishes and therefore, initially, zero-rated for quota.'

Another states that while no official strategy exists, the diocese is committed to maintaining its contribution via the Commissioners equalisation policy.

The strategies themselves cover a wide range of issues, varying from diocese to diocese. These include clergy deployment, church buildings, funding and other support of Church-based community projects, lay ministry, liturgy, theology, ecumenical working, inter-faith working, issues of race, new patterns of ministry, industry and the economy.

In general terms many show evidence of the current discussions about mutual support and interdependence, although methods for dealing with this vary, as the following contributions show:

> The strategy stresses the responsibility of every local church for its own ministry and for sharing responsibility where local churches, both urban and rural, are unable to do that fully themselves.

> The diocese has a strategy to support the urban Church in its own or other dioceses only inasmuch as it supported a £300,000 drive for the Church Urban Fund – we need to move from the charity syndrome to a strategic approach which involves the structures.

> Our Christian thinking, praying and action needs to be rooted in a real relationship with those in need, with the weak, the vulnerable and the powerless. This relationship will be one in which we have as much to receive as to give. This solidarity will be expressed not only through acts of individual kindness and generosity, but also by considering the major economic and political questions of our time from the point of view of their effect on the most disadvantaged.

Finance

Of the dioceses which responded:

17 operate some form of quota by potential scheme

1 is actively preparing a scheme

1 is considering the introduction of such a scheme

1 is moving partially away from such a system.

'Quota-by-potential' schemes are designed to take into account socio-economic factors in allocating parish shares, the contribution each parish makes towards diocesan costs in financing ministry, and other activities. They vary considerably as to how these figures are decided. Some have partial schemes (i.e. not merely schemes that take into account population, church membership and attendance etc.) with for example 40% of apportionments worked out on a 'giving-by-potential' basis. Some are worked out by looking at the income categories of members of the congregation; others by using Census data to determine a factor for the parish as a whole. In one diocese which responded there was no quota-by-potential scheme as such, but deaneries take economic factors into account in apportioning the deanery quota between parishes.

In another, there is no potential scheme but there are plans to diversify the quota system so that people and parishes can earmark funds for mission in community work.

Information was sought from link officers concerning the proportion of UPAs and non-UPAs which did not meet their quota commitments in full last year. Given the wide variations in numbers of UPAs between diocese, it would not be possible to make comparisons which made much sense. However, it is worth noting the situation in one diocese with substantial numbers of UPAs, where 45% of UPAs were unable to meet their commitments, but only 7% of non-UPAs failed to do so. This diocese has, in response to the clear discrepancies, decided to move to a quota-by-potential system to redress the balance.

Despite the financial pressures on dioceses, the recent growth in numbers of dioceses operating such schemes appears to be continuing. There are strong arguments for the development of such systems:

- they provide one method of cushioning the effects of the current financial crisis on poorer parishes

- they are demonstrations of the principle of interdependence across a diocese

- they allow churches in UPAs more financial security, thus enabling them to become genuinely local churches serving the deprived in their area.

But, above all, such systems are fairer than flat rate systems; in a Church which seeks justice, this is one challenge which tests our resolve and our pockets.

In response to the question 'how does the diocese plan to finance ministry in UPAs within the diocese five years hence?' most dioceses referred to their quota-by-potential schemes.

One link officer stated that assistance will be available within the parish shares scheme and supplementary grants, subject to the recommendation of the deaneries concerned.

Another pointed out that in his diocese, a Needs and Resources working party has produced a report, but that there are some thorny issues around. Some UPAs are arguing that their financial contribution (in funeral fees and in 'new' Christians who then move into the suburbs) is greater than the simple figures suggest. This should make us all wary about thinking of UPAs in terms solely of their needs; they should equally be valued as a rich resource, which in many cases shows itself in sacrificial levels of generosity (see also the Stewardship Committee's response in the Central Board of Finance review, chapter 4).

One link officer stated that there are no plans at present to do anything other than continue the existing policy. Any suggestion of change will be strongly resisted by the 140 UPA parishes in the diocese. This is one diocese where the needs of UPA parishes will not go unheard. Too often, the loudest voices in a diocese are those of large, successful and relatively wealthy congregations who push towards self-sufficiency and a narrow congregationalism. This illustrates the value in developing and nurturing the UPA voice, to ensure that the least powerful and the most financially vulnerable are able to be heard.

Finally, link officers were asked 'Is there an agreed diocesan statement acknowledging financial responsibility for UPAs in other dioceses?' None of the dioceses which responded claimed that there was. This may be because future arrangement for Commissioners' allocations to dioceses are as yet unknown; it is also true that dioceses are hard pressed to consider their own internal arrangements for financing ministry. However, this must be a priority for the next five years. There are such wide discrepancies between the relative wealth of dioceses that acknowledgement of responsibility for the poorer dioceses will be essential if the principle of interdependence is to survive across diocesan boundaries.

The role of the link officer

Twenty six link officers responded to this section. Of these:

6 had been in post for up to three years

7 for between 3 and 5 years

13 for between 5 and 10 years

Regarding hours:

6 spend up to 4 hours a week on link officer duties

8 between 4 and 8 hours

2 between 8 and 20 hours

4 between 20 and 40 hours

One harassed link officer spends sixty hours a week on his work. Others found their work so interwoven with their other responsibilities that they found it difficult to determine how long they spent.

The link officer role is usually combined with one or more post in the diocese. Of those responding:

6 were also spending substantial time on projects work, as projects officers

10 act as social responsibility officers

11 are part-time parish priests

1 is an archdeacon

4 are cathedral canons

3 are missioners

3 have responsibility for *Faith in the Countryside*

1 is director of ordinands

1 is responsible for Continuing Ministerial Education.

There is a great deal of variation between the levels of budgets available for link officer work:

8 absorb the costs under other budget headings

6 have budgets of under £500

4 have budgets of between £500 and £1,000

5 budgets of over £1,000

Other respondents offered no figures

When link officers were asked whether they were likely to be replaced, should they leave post:

3 said that it was unlikely

11 said probably

5 said definitely.

When asked whether they organised regular meetings for UPA clergy and laity in their diocese:

16 did so for clergy

11 did so for lay people

Link officers considered how frequently they were in contact with other key people within the diocesan structures; they responded as follows:

	FREQUENTLY	OCCASIONALLY	NEVER
Diocesan bishop	12	11	1
Other bishops	8	12	2
Diocesan secretaries	12	10	1
Diocesan Board of Finance	5	12	4
Board of Social Responsibility	20	2	1
Board of Mission	41	4	3
Board of Ministry	41	4	6
Board of Education	21	4	5
Council for Christian Unity	2	9	7
Church Urban Fund Projects officer	9	2	2
Officers of other denominations	4	13	5
Other faith leaders	11	3	8
Representatives of Black Anglican Concerns	6	7	9
Local authorities	11	9	2
Training and Enterprise Councils	3	9	10
MPs	3	9	10
Government regional offices	11	1	9
Inner Cities Religious Council	16	1	3

Groupings

It is clear from these results that the majority of the link officers have good contact with their diocesan bishop; this perhaps reflects the change in role of the *Faith in the City* work, with the now established annual reports from BAGUPA to the House of Bishops. This in effect gives BAGUPA two ways in to the diocese, through the link officers network and the House of Bishops.

The diocesan body with which most link officers had a clear and frequent relationship was the Board for Social Responsibility. This is probably due to the fact that several link officers are also social responsibility officers (see above), but it also reflects a general understanding that *Faith in the City* was essentially an act of the Church's social responsibility. This was certainly true but, as was shown by the results of the Board reviews, the life and work of the UPA Church has much wider implications for the Church.

Only five link officers had frequent contact with diocesan Boards of Finance; yet this is the area in which much closer relationships must develop. Link officers have expertise and experience in the sorts of issues which will be concerning Boards at present; they also have access to examples of what other dioceses are doing to protect UPA ministry.

It is interesting, moreover, that so many link officers have frequent contact with local authorities and voluntary organisations. Link officers are often able to lever large sums of money into the diocese.

The development of relationships with secular bodies also points to a growing acceptance of the Church as a key player in urban regeneration. It presents a model both of outreach, and also of understanding how God is at work in the secular world.

Appendix 3
Who's giving?

Article by Gill Moody, Bishops' Officer for UPAs,
reproduced from *Full Measure*, May 1995

> Taken overall, levels of personal giving are low in the
> Church of England, averaging barely £1 a week per church
> member. This average obscures wide differences from place
> to place. Statistical analysis suggests that, while giving per
> member is higher where employment and income levels are
> higher, the absolute amount given does not rise to the
> same extent as income rises. (7.63)

This extract from *Faith in the City* published ten years ago, highlights how
significant are the changes within the Church over that period.

We have seen a significant increase in the number of dioceses using
quota-by-potential schemes which take into account socio-economic
factors in determining appropriate weightings. We have seen a radical
challenge to the status quo brought about by the Church Commissioners'
financial difficulties. Levels of overall direct giving now stand at a weekly
average of £2.17 per electoral roll member.

Last year the Urban Bishops' Panel produced a paper for the House of
Bishops entitled 'Protecting Priority Areas'. This called for clear decisions
about financing ministry across the country, incorporating an element of
protection for poorer parishes and for dioceses with substantial concentrations of urban priority areas.

Within this context, there are three questions which I would want to
address to those concerned with stewardship; these questions are born out
of current perceptions of urban priority areas, perceptions of both their
needs and their rich resources.

Missionary congregations or 'first aid centres'

The Stewardship Committee of the Central Board of Finance recently
stated that 'Christian Stewardship guards against congregationalism and
encourages individual and parish to support one another through inter-

dependence. Systems that apportion diocesan costs so that the strong can help the weak are to be encouraged' and, with the reduced ability 'of the Church Commissioners to help the poorer dioceses, the Church does need a mechanism to ensure that appropriate help crosses diocesan boundaries.'

The Church Commissioners are presently exploring a number of options which may enable this to happen. Whatever is proposed, there must be an element of structural financial interdependence which will enable urban priority areas (and other poorer parishes) to be active in mission without having to rely either on particular acts of generosity from the wealthier churches, or on a bidding process which fails to allow churches financial security from year to year. Robert Warren, in his recent publication, suggests that developing missionary congregations should be a longer term strategic process, spanning six or seven years. Parishes in receipt of revenue funding from trusts for particular pieces of work will be aware of how crippling it can be to have to go through grant-making processes year in year out; how lack of financial security can damage long-term planning and lead to an atmosphere of crisis management.

Unless long-term strategies and mechanisms are developed which allow UPA congregations financial stability, urban churches will become nothing more than casualty departments, moving from one crisis to another.

Recognising the need

Since *Faith in the City* was published it is reported that urban congregations often give as generously (if not more) per electoral roll member than many non-urban congregations. This is backed up by some statistical evidence.

However, it is generally recognised that people who are poor, who have very limited disposable income, are often amongst the most generous givers, both to the Church and to other organisations. One woman I know, who worships in a South London congregation, survives on State Benefit. She has four children, one of whom is mentally ill, another physically disabled. She supports a live-in boyfriend and an ailing mother. Yet she has committed herself to giving £5 a week to the Church.

It is important to analyse why this should be the case. She is not an isolated case and it is not enough to simply point to her as a good example, a stick with which to beat wealthier congregations. Why does she give so much? I would suggest that it is for one very basic reason. This woman knows her need of God in a real and immediate way. For her the Church offers a salvation which is as important to her as food and clothing. This salvation touches her mind and her body; it touches her heart and soul and she gives with genuine willingness.

How might congregations where members are more comfortably off be challenged to recognise their need of God? We challenge them to respond to the needs of the poor, but how successfully do we help them discover their own need?

Who are the disciples?

The Church of England Stewardship Committee has stated that 'Christian Stewardship is about the discovering and use of human, material and spiritual resources to their best effect'. It also states that 'its major preoccupation is the fundamental teaching of discipleship to the whole Church'.

But whose resources? Who are the disciples?

Stewardship has traditionally been concerned with committed members as its base group (or target group in fundraising terms).

Ann Morisy from the London Diocese tells a story about a small congregation in a UPA who decided to open up a drop-in centre for the homeless on Sundays. Because of a shortage of volunteers from within the congregation, the planning group decided to open it up to the wider community. They advertised in the local press and three hundred people volunteered. If social action is an integral part of the Church's mission to the neighbourhood, then how can the Church respond effectively, in a missionary way, to those who offer resources to its work? Many congregations which, following *Faith in the City*, have organised projects to meet local needs, report the flourishing of discussion groups attended by those at varying stages of discipleship, by those who go to church regularly on a Sunday, and those who have never felt able to worship regularly. If we say that regular attendance at Sunday worship is the main criterion for measuring discipleship, then we are talking of a Church committed to maintenance rather than to mission.

Some have argued that it is too much to expect those peripherally involved with a church to contribute towards the costs of maintaining its ministry; others say that local non-churchgoers are often willing to pay for the costs of keeping a building but should not be approached to fund mainstream costs; others argue that if we widen our funding base we are relieving committed churchgoers of an essential aspect of this Christian responsibility. All these points carry weight, but are they symptomatic of a lack of confidence in the Gospel we proclaim? The Church is not just there for the benefit of regular committed members, but offers a lively Gospel of hope and redemption to the whole community. Are *we* generous enough to allow others to give; are we imaginative enough to develop ways of receiving?

A changing Church

We are in the middle of a period of radical change in the Church of England and it is important that we think creatively about stewardship if we are to be faithful to our Gospel. I suspect that the following might form the basis for ongoing discussion:

- is God at work only within committed Sunday congregations?

- what are our human, material and spiritual resources: those of committed churchgoers or those given by God to the whole of His creation? What model for stewardship best uses all of these gifts?

- what sort of Church do we want to be? What financial systems are appropriate to resource this Church? What sort of model for stewardship best serves this Church?

I am aware that others are asking these questions and that this is only one contribution to an on-going debate. However, it is time, at this tenth anniversary of *Faith in the City* for us to enter into the fray. The urban church has many pressing needs; it also has a wealth of wisdom and insight which deserves a wider hearing.

Appendix 4

Statistics

The Oxlip Index

The Oxlip Index is the successor to Z-scores as an identifier of the extent of deprivation within an area and as a means of identifying UPAs. The Index measures deprivation by estimating the proportion of the population (adults and children) within an area who are dependent on Income Support and Housing Benefit. As such it can be said to measure actual deprivation rather than vulnerability to deprivation (as was the case with Z-scores).

The Z-scores system was derived from the Department of Environment's Index of Deprivation, which was itself based on the 1981 Census; scores for benefices were built up from those of their component Enumeration Districts (EDs). When the DoE produced their new Index of Local Conditions, based on the 1991 Census and expressed in terms of Chi-scores, not all of the included indicators were available at ED level. The resulting attempt to make use of this Index for identifying UPAs was rejected as unsatisfactory by the dioceses.

The initial research involved in the development of the Oxlip Index was undertaken by staff within the Department of Applied Social Studies at Oxford University. Mike Noble, Tom Smith and their colleagues at Oxford had, for some time, been developing a method for using census data to quantify deprivation. Initially their formula depended on six of the census indicators, but the final version used just four. These were the number of unemployed, children living in unsuitable accommodation, children in low earning households and households with no cars.

The data they were working on related to EDs comprising wards in two local authority areas and they welcomed the opportunity to have their methods tested in other parts of the country. The model they had developed was adapted for the Church's use, applied to census data from benefices in six dioceses – with encouraging results – and finally tested more generally. After further fine-tuning, the Index was confirmed by a wide range of dioceses to be acceptable as a basis for identifying UPAs. Using the four census indicators listed above, the number of people in a benefice who are dependent on Income Support and Housing Benefit can be obtained.

A benefice for which it is estimated that 19 or more out of every 100 of its population are dependent on Income Support and Housing Benefit, is designated as having UPA status. Using this criterion approximately 14% of all benefices will be identified as areas of deprivation; under Z-scores there were 13%. The Church Urban Fund has accepted the use of Oxlip as a necessary part of the procedure it uses in the issuing of grants.

Computer programmes are supplied to the dioceses that will generate Oxlip scores, population figures and certain other census data for their benefices. However, before they can be used some painstaking work has to be done at diocesan level to identify accurately the geographical composition of benefices (the EDs which make up the benefice).

Whilst the present formula is seen as being both fair and flexible, the research is on-going. Oxlip is a means of sorting benefices into an order and further research will seek to refine the ordering process. One particular area for development lies in the identification of sizeable areas of deprivation within large benefices. A deprivation score for a benefice gives only a partial picture and access to the full range of census data would enable fuller benefice/parish profiles to be developed.

Table 1

Table 1 shows the situation as at the beginning of September 1995. For some dioceses the mapping of benefice boundaries will remain partial and has been restricted to those areas most likely to contain UPAs. For others the mapping exercise is still in progress and further UPA benefices will be identified.

As a separate exercise a 'Diocesan Oxlip score' has been calculated from a mapping of ward and civil boundaries. These scores are shown in the final column of table 1 and the dioceses are listed in the table in descending order of their Oxlip score.

125

Table 1: Information held on Oxlip database (September 1995)

DIOCESE	Number of benefices on the database	which are identified as UPAs to date :	Percentage of diocesan population included on the database (based on1991 Census)	Diocesan Oxlip score
London	382	195	98.3	21.18
Southwark	294	124	98.4	19.50
Liverpool	198	83	98.6	19.49
Birmingham	157	63	94.6	18.40
Manchester	287	119	97.7	18.37
Durham	235	67	98.5	17.98
Newcastle	126	32	87.9	17.47
Sheffield	163	54	98.6	17.08
Bradford	113	22	98.2	15.49
Ripon	125	27	97.3	14.85
Wakefield	171	27	97.5	14.47
York	282	39	96.7	14.36
Southwell	182	23	98.5	14.20
Chelmsford	361	47	96.6	13.58
Blackburn	118	39	64.6	13.19
Lichfield	322	38	98.5	13.06
Coventry	137	10	98.5	12.72
Portsmouth	117	13	90.5	12.27
Canterbury	152	11	98.1	12.21

Chester	193	26	77.9	12.20
Bristol	118	15	94.5	12.09
Lincoln	22	14	19.5	11.98
Exeter	151	20	76.5	11.92
Derby	187	12	98.1	11.82
Leicester	32	14	34.3	11.54
Truro				11.48
Chichester	1	1	1.1	11.19
Peterborough	45	12	55.4	11.08
Carlisle	173	7	98.1	11.01
Norwich	2	1	2.0	10.95
Worcester	Unlikely to participate this year			10.83
Rochester				10.51
Winchester	1	0	1.0	10.22*
St.Albans	74	9	36.2	9.90
Gloucester	166	6	98.1	9.60
Bath & Wells	1	0	1.4	9.52
Hereford	1	0	6.4	9.28
Salisbury	2	0	3.2	9.10
Ely	12	2	4.6	8.98
Oxford	3	1	1.9	8.97
St.Edms & Ipswich	Not participating			8.88
Guildford	147	0	95.3	7.49
Sodor & Man	Not participating			n/a

*excluding Channel Isles

Table 2

The definition of UPAs which is used in this table and tables 3 and 4 is based on the nationally consistent system of Z-scores which was derived from the former Index of Deprivation produced by the Department of the Environment. The population figures used in tables 2 and 3 are based on the 1981 Census, and they update, and in certain cases correct, information given in *Living Faith in the City* (LFITC).

The 20 dioceses that appeared in the corresponding table in *Living Faith in the City* are listed in the same order as they appeared there and the other dioceses are in alphabetic order.

Table 3

Columns A to E show numbers of full-time parochial stipendiary clergy in post at 1 January 1992 and are based on *Crockford's* listings at that date. Columns F to H respectively show the average population per clergy in the diocese as a whole, in UPA benefices only and in non-UPA benefices only. Column J gives a comparison of the ratio of population to clergy in the UPAs with that of the diocese as a whole. A positive figure indicates that the UPA clergy had more people in their care than is the case in the diocese as a whole, and a negative figure that they had fewer.

Column K makes asimilar comparison between staffing ratios in the UPAs and the non-UPAs, again as at 1 January 1992. A positive figure in this column indicates that the UPA benefices had a greater number of parishioners per clergy than the non-UPAs (i.e. a poorer staffing level), and a negative figure implies better staffing levels in the UPAs. Where available, comparisons with the 1989 and 1984 equivalents are given in columns L and M to indicate the trend over the three years since *Living Faith in the City* and the eight years since *Faith in the City*. If the column K entry is lower than those in columns M and N, then the 1992 staffing level shows a relative improvement from the earlier years.

The use of the number of clergy in post at a particular date reflects the reality of the situation on the ground but this figure will be affected by vagaries in the distribution of vacancies and the allocation of curates. Also in dioceses where there are relatively few UPA benefices comparisons of staffing levels between the UPAs and the non-UPAs may not be a statistically valid exercise.

Table 4

Direct giving is defined as the total of all moneys received from all planned giving schemes, church collections and boxes, but excludes income from special fund raising events, income tax refunds on covenants, net profits on sale of magazines etc. Membership is a an average of the adult Usual Sunday Attendance (USA) figure and the Electoral Roll figure which is weighted 2 to 1 in favour of the USA. For the purpose of the comparison the total direct giving is averaged out over the total membership and given as a weekly amount. Details of membership and finance were extracted from the 1993 parishes returns where such returns had been submitted. It should be noted particularly that where membership is small comparisons of giving levels should be viewed with caution. No attempt is made to comment on these statistics other than to say that they warrant further research and that it would be appropriate to repeat the exercise using data for other years.

It would be appropriate to make the comment that once the exercise of identifying UPAs under Oxlip has been completed, then the way lies open to repeating and extending previously conducted research which compared UPA and non-UPA benefices.

Table 2: UPA population comparisons (updating appendix D of *Living Faith in the City*)

DIOCESE (20 "urban diocese in LFITC order")	Total population in: Diocese	UPAs	percentage of diocesan population in UPAs	Number of benefices which are: in the diocese	recognised as UPAs	percentage of benefices which are UPAs	Average benefice population for: whole diocese	UPAs	Non-UPAs
London	3,129,210	1,442,035	46.1%	416	176	42.3%	7,522	8,193	7,030
Liverpool	1,627,334	733,359	45.1%	202	80	39.6%	8,056	9,167	7,328
Birmingham	1,420,679	738,479	52.0%	161	81	50.3%	8,824	9,117	8,528
Manchester	1,965,209	897,062	45.6%	291	124	42.6%	6,753	7,234	6,396
Southwark	2,221,719	959,784	43.2%	297	120	40.4%	7,481	7,998	7,130
Bradford	616,182	234,316	38.0%	113	26	23.0%	5,453	9,012	4,389
Ripon	741,563	231,864	31.3%	126	25	19.8%	5,885	9,275	5,047
Coventry	744,362	227,086	30.5%	138	20	14.5%	5,394	11,354	4,384
Lichfield	2,047,703	586,430	28.6%	342	57	16.7%	5,987	10,288	5,127
York	1,269,008	337,613	26.6%	281	29	10.3%	4,516	11,642	3,696
Leicester	805,059	223,626	27.8%	142	22	15.5%	5,669	10,165	4,845
Sheffield	1,178,263	300,673	25.5%	160	33	20.6%	7,364	9,111	6,910
Durham	1,492,119	375,367	25.2%	236	43	18.2%	6,323	8,729	5,786
Blackburn	1,220,677	318,628	26.1%	221	46	20.8%	5,523	6,927	5,155
Newcastle	765,915	151,358	19.8%	133	18	13.5%	5,759	8,409	5,344
Chelmsford	2,499,156	491,981	19.7%	374	45	12.0%	6,682	10,933	6,101
Southwell	984,606	178,059	18.1%	181	22	12.2%	5,440	8,094	5,073
Chester	1,537,045	273,307	17.8%	244	29	11.9%	6,299	9,424	5,878
Bristol	778,080	107,832	13.9%	125	12	9.6%	6,225	8,986	5,931
Wakefield	1,044,176	174,425	16.7%	174	25	14.4%	6,001	6,977	5,837
For all 20 "urban dioceses"	28,088,065	8,983,284	32.0%	4,357	1,033	23.7%	6,447	8,696	5,748

Diocese									
Bath and Wells	736,636			222			3,318		3,318
Canterbury	734,301	26,457	3.6%	155	4	2.6%	4,737	6,614	4,688
Carlisle	468,581	18,950	4.0%	177	2	1.1%	2,647	9,475	2,569
Chichester	1,300,007	44,942	3.5%	305	7	2.3%	4,262	6,420	4,212
Derby	927,107	66,145	7.1%	188	11	5.9%	4,931	6,013	4,864
Ely	508,255	76,975	8.3%	259	13	5.2%	1,962	5,921	1,962
Exeter	929,151	4,520	0.9%	251	1	0.6%	3,702	4,520	3,581
Gloucester*	526,395			167			3,152		3,144
Guildford	872,163			151			5,776		5,776
Hereford	257,351	16,168	6.3%	147	1	0.7%	1,751	16,168	1,652
Lincoln	851,050	109,739	12.9%	286	7	2.4%	2,976	15,677	2,657
Norwich	706,947			237			2,983		2,983
Oxford*	1,748,756	45,673	2.6%	343	4	1.2%	5,098	11,418	5,024
Peterborough	655,472	80,479	12.3%	171	11	6.4%	3,833	7,316	3,594
Portsmouth	647,946	12,449	1.9%	124	3	2.4%	5,225	4,150	5,252
Rochester	1,145,009	93,431	8.2%	192	12	6.3%	5,964	7,786	5,842
St Albans	1,486,718	78,008	5.2%	241	10	4.1%	6,169	7,801	6,098
St Edms and Ipswich	521,628	8,358	1.6%	187	1	0.5%	2,789	8,358	2,760
Salisbury	724,391			188			3,853		3,853
Sodor & Man	65,240			28			2,330		2,330
Truro	419,174	23,983	5.7%	143	4	2.8%	2,931	5,996	2,843
Winchester	923,617	68,020	7.4%	211	8	3.8%	4,377	8,503	4,215
Worcester	605,485	48,273	8.0%	113	5	4.4%	5,358	9,655	5,159
All dioceses	45,849,445	9,805,854	21.4%	8,843	1,137	12.9%	5,185	8,624	4,677

*excludes other possible UPAs for which available data appear to cover only part of the benefice.

131

Table 3: Comparison of direct giving levels in UPA and non-UPA parishes

DIOCESE	UPA parishes		non-UPA parishes	
	Number of members	average direct giving (per week)	Number of members	average direct giving (per week)
LONDON	12,808	£4.37	27,318	£5.40
MANCHESTER	10,128	£3.11	18,751	£3.13
SOUTHWARK	8,716	£4.48	22,390	£4.88
LIVERPOOL	7,826	£2.80	19,714	£2.77
BIRMINGHAM	5,698	£3.56	9,933	£4.26
LICHFIELD	5,301	£3.07	28,815	£2.91
All dioceses with over 5,000 UPA members	50,477	£3.66	126,921	£3.91
BLACKBURN	4,746	£3.07	27,364	£2.51
DURHAM	4,226	£2.57	18,227	£2.66
CHESTER	3,125	£2.83	34,222	£2.97
CHELMSFORD	2,567	£3.07	30,226	£3.35
RIPON	2,564	£3.77	13,859	£2.59
YORK	2,086	£3.40	23,999	£2.70
LEICESTER	2,061	£3.41	11,723	£3.55
SHEFFIELD	2,023	£3.24	15,182	£3.31
All dioceses with UPA membership over 2,000 but under 5,000	23,398	£3.10	174,802	£2.93
BRADFORD	1,989	£3.97	8,760	£3.92
COVENTRY	1,955	£2.66	11,002	£2.84
WAKEFIELD	1,579	£2.82	11,736	£2.86
ROCHESTER	1,488	£4.48	21,582	£3.66
NEWCASTLE	1,311	£2.87	11,816	£3.29

SOUTHWELL	1,266	£3.97	12,325	£4.72
WINCHESTER	1,099	£3.10	30,151	£2.68
All dioceses with UPA membership over 1,000 but under 2,000	10,687	£3.41	107,372	£3.32
PETERBOROUGH	925	£3.43	15,052	£3.14
ST ALBANS	873	£3.30	33,200	£3.34
CHICHESTER	868	£2.91	43,435	£2.73
LINCOLN	863	£2.01	14,613	£2.20
DERBY	773	£4.14	15,073	£3.21
BRISTOL	739	£2.62	15,104	£3.72
WORCESTER	615	£2.64	15,052	£2.53
All dioceses with UPA membership over 500 but under 1,000	5,656	£3.02	151,529	£2.98
CANTERBURY	444	£3.76	16,074	£3.33
TRURO	365	£2.55	12,128	£2.17
CARLISLE	346	£3.10	16,322	£2.77
PORTSMOUTH	167	£2.48	12,835	£2.99
HEREFORD	135	£2.35	9,322	£2.54
ST EDS & IPSWICH	104	£2.26	18,602	£2.83
GLOUCESTER	41	£2.71	19,105	£2.94
OXFORD	28	£3.92	38,603	£3.57
EXETER	18	£4.08	26,512	£2.67
SODOR & MAN			1,278	£2.77
GUILDFORD			25,551	£4.07
ELY			15,246	£2.63
SALISBURY			29,269	£2.58
NORWICH			20,769	£2.79
BATH & WELLS			30,584	£2.93
All dioceses with under 500 UPA members	1,648	£2.99	292,200	£3.00
ALL DIOCESES	91,866	£3.44	852,824	£3.16

Table 4: Clergy deployment comparisons

DIOCESE (20 "urban diocese in LFITC order)	Parochial Stipendiary clergy (in post at January 1992)					Population per clergy			Differences:			
	(A) Men	(B) Women	(C) TOTAL	(D) UPA	(E) Non-UPA	(F) All benefices	(G) UPA benefices	(H) Non-UPA benefices	(J) between UPA and total	(K) between UPA & non-UPA in: Jan 1992	(L) Early 1989 (LFITC)	(M) c. 1984 (FITC)
London	534	37	571	250	321	5,480	5,768	5,256	5%	10%	22%	25%#
Liverpool	252	19	271	129	142	6,005	5,685	6,296	-5%	-10%	-10%	5%
Birmingham	191	13	204	104	100	6,964	7,101	6,822	2%	4%	13%	16%
Manchester	327	14	341	155	186	5,763	5,787	5,743	nil	1%	-3%	nil
Southwark	370	37	407	184	223	5,459	5,216	5,659	-4%	-8%	-1%	-3%
Bradford	116	10	126	35	91	4,890	6,695	4,196	37%	60%	61%	75%
Ripon	148	16	164	45	119	4,522	5,153	4,283	14%	20%	16%	29%
Coventry	153	10	163	32	131	4,567	7,096	3,949	55%	80%	62%	87%
Lichfield	376	27	403	96	307	5,081	6,109	4,760	20%	28%	34%	25%
York	298	23	321	47	274	3,953	7,183	3,399	82%	111%	102%	25%
Leicester	166	8	174	39	135	4,627	5,734	4,307	24%	33%	24%	
Sheffield	197	17	214	47	167	5,506	6,397	5,255	16%	22%	17%	
Durham	265	17	282	71	211	5,291	5,287	5,293	nil	nil	11%	
Blackburn	251	7	258	59	199	4,731	5,400	4,533	14%	19%	12%	32%
Newcastle	160	6	166	27	139	4,614	5,606	4,421	21%	27%	19%	35%
Chelmsford	450	23	473	71	402	5,284	6,929	4,993	31%	39%	34%	
Southwell	195	12	207	35	172	4,757	5,087	4,689	7%	8%	6%	
Chester	295	12	307	43	264	5,007	6,356	4,787	27%	33%	32%	
Bristol	141	16	157	16	141	4,956	6,740	4,754	36%	42%	23%	
Wakefield	187	12	199	34	165	5,247	5,130	5,271	-2%	-3%	7%	1%
For all 20 "urban dioceses"	5,072	336	5,408	1,519	3,889	5,194	5,914	4,913	14%	20%	21%	

134

Bath and Wells	240	13	253		253	2,912	4,410	2,912	7%	7%
Canterbury	168	10	178	6	172	4,125	6,317	4,115	124%	129%
Carlisle	159	7	166	3	163	2,823	3,457	2,758	-9%	-9%
Chichester	337	7	344	13	331	3,779	4,725	3,792	7%	7%
Derby	195	14	209	14	195	4,436		4,415		
Ely	149	8	157		157	3,237	3,665	3,237	12%	13%
Exeter	273	10	283	21	262	3,283	4,520	3,253	58%	58%
Gloucester*	171	13	184	1	183	2,861		2,852		
Guildford	184	16	200		200	4,361	8,084	4,361		
Hereford	121	5	126	2	124	2,042		1,945	296%	316%
Lincoln	228	17	245	16	229	3,474	6,859	3,237	97%	112%
Norwich	219	10	229		229	3,087		3,087		
Oxford*	427	35	462	8	454	3,785	5,709	3,751	51%	52%
Peterborough	171	10	181	16	165	3,621	5,030	3,485	39%	44%
Portsmouth	125	7	132	2	130	4,909	6,225	4,888	27%	27%
Rochester	214	17	231	17	214	4,957	5,496	4,914	11%	12%
St Albans	282	25	307	13	294	4,843	6,001	4,792	24%	25%
St Edms and Ipswich	187	8	195	1	194	2,675	8,358	2,646	212%	216%
Salisbury	237	12	249		249	2,909		2,909		
Sodor & Man	18	0	18		18	3,624		3,624		
Truro	132	3	135	5	130	3,105	4,797	3,040	54%	58%
Winchester	231	7	238	14	224	3,881	4,859	3,820	25%	27%
Worcester	131	11	142	8	134	4,284	6,034	4,158	42%	45%
All dioceses	9,671	601	10,272	1,679	8,593	4,464	5,840	4,195	31%	39%

London published figure of +7% in Faith in the City excluded City of London churches

Appendix 5

Bibliography

Faith in the City and related publications

Faith in the City, the report of the Archbishop of Canterbury's Commission on Urban Priority Areas, Church House Publishing, 1985, fifth impression with index, 1989.

Faith in the City, the popular version, Christian Action, 1985.

It's for You, a study guide to *Faith in the City*, Board of Education, 1986. Available from Church House Bookshop.

Gallup Survey of Church of England Clergymen, prepared for the Archbishop's Commission on Urban Priority Areas, 1986. Available from Church House Bookshop.

An Audit for the Local Church, Board for Mission and Unity, 1986. Available from Church House Bookshop.

Discovering Faith in the City, a pamphlet for those not living in UPAs, the Advisory Group on *Faith in the City*, Church House Publishing, 1988.

Towards Partnership, proposals for the establishment of local church/civic/community forums, the Advisory Group on *Faith in the City*, 1988. Available from the Bishops' Officer for UPAs.

Linking Up, a guide to church links, the Advisory Group on *Faith in the City*, 1989. Available from the Bishops' Offficer for UPAs.

Through the Eyes of the Clergy, report of a survey comparing the attitudes and ministerial experiences of UPA and non-UPA clergy. Prepared for the Bishops' Advisory Group on Urban Priority Areas. Forthcoming.

Ahern G and Davie G, *Inner City God: the nature of belief in the inner city*, Hodder & Stoughton, 1987.

Blakeborough E, *Church for the City*, Darton, Longman and Todd, 1995.

Green L, *Power to the Powerless*, Marshall Pickering, 1987.

Russell H, *Poverty Close to Home: The Political and Theological Challenge of Poverty in Britain*, Mowbrays, 1995.

Vincent J, *Situation Analysis* 1978; *Starting All Over Again*, WCC, 1981; *Into the City*, Epworth, 1982; *Radical Jesus*, Marshall Pickering, 1986; *Britain in the 90s*, Methodist Publishing House, 1989; *British Liberation Theology* (forthcoming).

J Jones and J Langley (eds), *Social Policy and the City*, Avebury (1995).

136

REFERENCES

Chapter 1

Figure 3 from *Households Below Average Income,* Crown copyright, reproduced with the permission of the Controller of HMSO.

Robson B et al *Assessing the Impact of Urban Policy,* (1994). Crown copyright, reproduced with the permission of the Controller of HMSO.

Willmott P (ed.), *Urban Trends 1 and 2,* Policy Studies Institute 1992 and 1994.

Barclay, Sir Peter (Chairman), *Income and Wealth,* Vols 1 & 2, Joseph Rowntree Foundation 1995.

Benzeval M, Judge K, Whitehead M (Eds), *Tackling Inequalities in Health,* The King's Fund 1995.

Borrie Sir Gordon (Chairman), *Social Justice: Strategies for National Renewal,* Vintage 1994.

Walton J (Lord Walton of Dechant), *Learning to Succeed,* Heinemann 1993.

Thornton, Sir Malcolm (Chairman), *Performance in City Schools: Third Report of the Education Committee of the House of Commons, Session 1994-995.* Crown copyright, reproduced with the permission of the Controller of HMSO.

Stern Vivian, *Crime Policy and the Role of Punishment,* the Journal of the Royal Society for the Encouragement of Arts, Manufactures and Commerce, vol CXLI No. 5443 October 1993.

Saunders L and Stradling B, *From School to Work: a Decade of Initiatives,* Policy Studies vol. 15 No.3 Autumn 1994.

Wells J, *Crime and Unemployment,* Employment Policy Institute Economic Report vol. 9 No.1, February 1995.

Power A and Tunstall R, *Swimming against the tide: Polarisation or progress on, 20 unpopular council estates 1980-95,* Joseph Rowntree Foundation 1995; *People Need Homes: A National Programme of Local Research and Action on Housing and Homelessness,* Churches National Housing Coalition 1995.

Shiner P, *Local Work,* Centre for Local and Economic Strategies 1995.

Griffiths S, *How Housing Benefit can work for community care,* Joseph Rowntree Foundation 1995.

Clark G, *A Missed Opportunity,* National Council for Voluntary Organisations 1995.

Goodman A and Webb S, *The Distribution of UK Household Expenditure 1979-92,* The Institute for Fiscal Studies 1995.

Webb S, *Poverty Dynamics in Great Britain: Preliminary Analysis from the British Household Panel Survey,* The Institute for Fiscal Studies 1995.

OTHER REFERENCES

Board for Social Responsibility

Not Just for the Poor: Christian Perspectives on the Welfare State, report of the Social Policy Committee of the Board for Social Responsibility, Church House Publishing, 1986.

Church and Community Work: A response to Faith in the City, Report of a Working Party of the Social Policy Committee, BSR, 1988.

Something to Celebrate: Valuing Families in Church and Society, the report of a Working Party of the Board for Social Responsibility, Church House Publishing, 1995.

Board of Education

Grant-Maintained Status and the Church, Board of Education, the National Society, 1991.

All God's Children, Board of Education, the National Society/Church House Publishing, 1991.

Advisory Board of Ministry

Education for the Church's Ministry: the report of the Working Party on Assessment, the Advisory Council for the Church's Ministry, Occasional Paper No.22, CBF, 1987.

Before You Leap: A practical guide to ministers about moving to an inner city parish, the Advisory Council for the Church's Ministry, Occasional Paper No.28, CBF, 1988.

Theology in Practice: the proposals of the ACCM Working Party on Urban Studies Centres, the Advisory Council for the Church's Ministry, Occasional Paper No. 29, CBF, 1988.

Facing the Challenge of Racism: Story, Reflection and Practice in Theological Education and Training, Goodrich S, Parsons S and Richardson R (eds), the Advisory Board for Ministry in association with the Runnymede Trust, ABM Ministry Paper No.8. CBF, 1994.

A Review of Selection Procedures in the Church of England: the report of a Working Party the Advisory Board of Ministry, ABM Policy Paper No. 6. CBF, 1995.

General Synod Office

Working as One Body, the report of the Archbishops' Comission on the Organisation of the Church of England, Church House Publishing, 1995.

Quota Workshops: a report and support documents, the Stewardship Committee, CBF, 1993.

Church Statistics: some facts and figures about the Church of England, CBF, annually.

Board of Mission

Finding Faith Today, Finney J, the Bible Society and Churches Together in England, 1992.

Being Human, Being Church, Warren R, Harper Collins, 1995.

Time for Sharing, Board of Mission, 1995.

Breaking New Ground: Church Planting in the Church of England (GS Misc 1099), report by a Working Party of the Board of Mission, Church House Publishing, 1994.

The Gospel as Public Truth for London, Richards A. Available from the Board of Mission.

Multi-faith Worship, the Inter-faith Committee of the Board of Mission, Church House Publishing, 1992.

Faith in the Countryside, a report presented to the Archbishops of Canterbury and York, Churchman Publishing, 1990.

Doctrine Commission

The Mystery of Salvation, report by the Doctrine Commission, Church House Publishing, 1995.

Liturgical Commission

The Renewal of Common Prayer: Unity and Diversity in Church of England Worship, (GS Misc 412), Perham M (ed.), essays by the Liturgical Commission, Church House Publishing/SPCK, 1993.

Patterns for Worship, the Liturgical Commission, commended edition, Church House Publishing, 1995.

Committee for Black Anglican Concerns

Seeds of Hope: Report of a Survey on Instruments for Combating Racism in the Dioceses of the Church of England (GS 977), the Committee for Black Anglican Concerns, the General Synod of the Church of England, 1991.

How We Stand: a Report on Black Membership of the Church of England in the 1990s, the Committee for Black Anglican Concerns, the General Synod of the Church of England, 1994.

Council for the Care of Churches

Mission in Mortar: the role of the church building in the Decade of Evangelism (GS1073), the Council for the Care of Churches, the General Synod of the Church of England, 1993.

Church Urban Fund

Stories of Hope, Church Urban Fund publicity material, 1992-94.

Hope in the City? the local impact of the Church Urban Fund, Farnell R et al, CRESR, Sheffield Hallam University, 1994.

Broad-Based Organising: an Evaluation for the Church Urban Fund, Farnell R et al, CRESR, Sheffield Hallam University, 1994.

Report of the *Hope in the City?* Working Party, Church Urban Fund, 1995.

Urban Theology Group

God in the City: Essays and reflections from Archbishop of Canterbury's Urban Theology Group. Sedgwick P, (ed.), Mowbrays, 1995.

Churches National Housing Coalition

Churches and Housing Handbook, The Churches National Housing Coalition, 1994.

Rent Guarantee Schemes Handbook, The Churches National Housing Coalition, 1993.

Department of the Environment

Our Future Homes, Department of the Environment. HMSO, 1995.

Church Action on Poverty

Hearing the Cry of the Poor, A Declaration by Church Action on Poverty, CAP, 1989.

Church Action on Poverty Newsletter, Church Action on Poverty, periodical.

Voice Box, Church Action on Poverty, periodical.

Churches Commission for Racial Justice

One Race: a study pack for churches on racial violence, Churches Commission for Racial Justice, 1994.

Urban Theology Unit

Stirrings, Urban Theology Unit. Epworth, 1976

Gospel from the Poor, Urban Theology Unit, UTU, 1984.

Good News in Britain, Urban Theology Unit, UTU 1994.

Two Nations, One Gospel, Methodist Church/UTU, 1993.

Glossary and list of abbreviations

ABM	Advisory Board of Ministry (formerly ACCM)
ACORA	Archbishop's Commission on Rural Areas
ACUPA	Archbishop's Commission on Urban Priority Areas
BAGUPA	Bishops' Advisory Group on Urban Priority Areas
BoE	Board of Education
BoM	Board of Mission
BSR	Board for Social Responsibility
CAP	Church Action on Poverty
CBAC	Committee on Black Anglican Concerns
CBF	Central Board of Finance
CCBI	Council of Churches for Britain and Ireland
CCRJ	Churches Commission for Racial Justice
CCT	Churches Conservation Trust
Chi-score	Nearly, but not quite, the new Index of Deprivation
CME	Continuing Ministerial Education
CNHC	Churches National Housing Coalition
CUF	Church Urban Fund
DAC	Diocesan Advisory Committee
DBF	Diocesan Board of Finance
ED	Enumeration District
EUF	Ecumenical Urban Forum
FITC	*Faith in the City* (published 1985)
GP	General Practitioner
GS	General Synod
GS MISC	General Synod Miscellaneous Paper
HITC	*Hope in the City* report by Sheffield Hallam University

ICRC	Inner Cities Religious Council
IMCGB	International Ministerial Council of Great Britain
LEA	Local Education Authority
LEP	Local Ecumenical Partnership
LFITC	Living Faith in the City (published 1990)
NS	National Society
Oxlip	Oxford Low Income Prediction (new Index of Deprivation)
PCC	Parochial Church Council
UPA	Urban Priority Area
USA	Usual Sunday Attendance
UTU	Urban Theology Unit
Z-scores	former Index of Deprivation